The Return of

Jesus
My
King
2016

The Story of God's Clock

Roger F. La Rose

First Print
April 1999

Second Print
May 2011

©1999
Matthew C. Cox

All rights reserved. No part of this book may be used or reproduced in any manner whatsoever without written permission of the Matthew C. Cox, except in the case of brief quotations embodied in critical articles and reviews. For information contact

>Matthew C. Cox
>21 Pine Ridge Road
>Sandia Park, NM
>87047 505-286-9567
>mccox@comcast.net

Scripture references are taken from the HOLY BIBLE, NEW INTERNATIONAL VERSION®. Copyright© 1973,1978,1984 by International Bible Society. Used by permission of Zondervan Publishing House. All rights reserved. The "NIV" and "New International Version" trademarks are registered in the United States Patent and Trademark Office by International Bible Society. Use of either trademark requires the permission of International Bible Society.

Scripture references are also taken from King James Authorized Version 1611.

(References are from NIV unless otherwise noted.)

Library of Congress Control Number: 2011906542

ISBN-13: 978-0615483474

ISBN-10: 061548347X

Published by Peace of Mind Training Institute Publishing

Sandia Park, NM

Foreword

Roger LaRose was a unique servant of Jesus. Although his time in that role was rather brief, he accomplished a great deal and touched the lives of many people. He personally led a substantial number to faith in Jesus and some to a better immediate life on earth as well. He wrote this book as a sideline to his ministry. It did not begin as a project to write a book at all. It started simply as a personal inquiry into some statements in the Scripture which he found personally intriguing.

It was during the time of his devout study and work with the men who came to Gadarenes that Roger began to be particularly fascinated by two things, which turned out to be integrally related. The first was the Biblical concept of "Rest". The second was the Precision of Scripture. Roger noticed that the scripture normally only states the month or year of a given event. Occasionally, when the scripture specifies the day, he suspected that this indicated something special. As he pursued this idea, he discovered vast new insights.

He was particularly interested in the way some dates are precisely specified, while most are not so precise. This interest seems to have blossomed in response to a Palm Sunday sermon when he heard the calculation of the date of the Triumphal entry into Jerusalem as given by Josh McDowell in Evidence That Demands a Verdict (p. 181). Shortly after that sermon, Roger began researching precise dates and intervals.

Over the next year or so Roger gained new insights. They finally became so numerous that he was encouraged to collect them all into a magazine article, or perhaps for a tract or pamphlet. As he began to do this, the "article" grew beyond the original concept. Finally, it became clear that a book was in process.

Roger began to write and God used those around him to finance the initial transformation of his notes and text into printed form. The development continued until Roger's unexpected death in November of 1997.

For the most part, this text is presented essentially as he left it. Some themes were not quite completed, and he had many more that he had shared with those around him. These will remain for the reader to discover and carry farther, under the direction of the Holy Spirit.

Roger had skills and talents which uniquely qualified him to write this book. He was employed by a large technology company for much of his life. Even though his education included a master's degree in Physics, his specialty was the design of large-scale computer operating systems and networks. It is easy to see why he had such a fascination with numbers and the way in which the Bible presents them.

It is important to realize a few premises which form the basis of Roger's analysis. Roger accepted the Bible, as God's direct revelation of Himself to man, without error or contradiction. He accepted it in that way because he realized that if the Bible contained error or contradiction, that it would be completely beyond man's ability to sort out the truth from the error. Apparent contradictions were seen as incomplete understanding on our part and hence, as opportunities for new insights. Even though Roger was a man of formidable intellect and widely read, he realized that no one can understand the Bible from a solely intellectual point of view. He relied upon interpretation by the Holy Spirit to help him easily derive error from truth.

During the time of intense study that he spent after his conversion his studies led him to accept the basic premises of the eschatological position known as "Pre-millennianism". But, he did not accept the concept of "Dispensations", which is often attached to "Pre-millennianism". He also directed much of his study toward the "Rapture" question, since it is integrally related with "Rest" and precision in dating. In all this, he never seemed to take an established position and defend it. He was merely open to insights as they were revealed during his study.

Consequently, this book was not written to espouse a particular position of theological treatise, but more a record of discoveries. It should, in my opinion, be read more as a diary or research notebook, such as any scientist or research engineer would keep in his daily work, than as a finished scholarly paper. Most of Roger's insights are recorded here. Though he was unable to see the actual completion of the book, it is clear that the One Who gave the insights and revelations knew exactly how much time Roger had and is Himself never late nor lacking. The book must, therefore, be regarded as complete!

The clear implication of the 2016 focus is that we must diligently be about the work He has assigned to each of us. Much turmoil and uncertainty seems to be in the near future. Many need to hear the message that we can enter into His Rest, even today! Until the culmination comes Jesus is our Sabbath Rest. Then He completes even that.

Enjoy this book. Puzzle over it. Question every part of it. That is the manner of a real seeker of Truth. Roger LaRose was one of those true seekers. He found the real Truth to be the Word, Jesus Christ. He now fully understands "Rest". May you find Truth and Rest for yourself in Him.

Ronald L. Woodfin, Ph.D., Pastor
Cedar Crest Baptist Church
Cedar Crest, New Mexico
September 25, 1998

A Note from the Editor
By Sheri Cox

At Roger's request, I had the privilege of working with him on this book. We worked many days and hours to get it as close as possible to how he wanted it to read, as the Lord led him. (The beginning stages were slow, so, as Dr. Woodfin shares in the foreword, Cedar Crest Baptist Church financed putting the initial work into printed form.)

Just a few weeks before his death we were very close to the completion of the book. He had noted in the latest draft the changes that we were to make next. The changes he made are reflected in this present edition. It also includes, to the best of my ability, what he called the "Error Analysis", which had to be derived from his hand written notes.

We have not changed the spacing in the book, leaving it somewhat awkward in actual appearance. It was Roger's desire that each one should discern for himself what God was showing him in this, therefore I have felt led that the spacing should remain as is. Please use this "extra space" for notes as God gives you insights on what you read here.

I learned a great deal during the writing of this book and still have much to learn. I pray God will bless you and help you to grow in His ways as you read and study.

PREFACE

In a very few years two prophets will appear on the earth. They will have a message from God - but that message <u>will not</u> be received. If that message is for the world, these men will be hated and ridiculed and put to death.

And then <u>that</u> world will end! (Praise God!)

If the message is for the church, will these men be hated and ridiculed and put to death? ....perhaps!

And then <u>that</u> church will end! (Praise God!)

Could this be?

This text is the story of Jesus' kingdom and the time of its coming...the precise time of its coming. God has set this "time" and it will not change. God has given us His precise prediction of when that kingdom will come. It should have come already - but hasn't. The "time of its coming" hasn't changed - God simply changed "time".

This is the story of God's clock.

Acknowledgments

Some special thanks are in order:

Firstly to my Mom and Dad who provided the cloister for and bore the artistic ravings of the handwritten experience - for tolerance 'above and beyond' I thank you. May Jesus fill your heart and home…forever.

And to Joyce who first showed me a picture of Jesus.

Also to Ron and Martha who have led and loved and taught by living what was bought.

And to Jerry and DaVonna and John for sharing some of the first steps along "THE WAY".

And most of all to Matt and Sheri who pushed all the right buttons (some more than once!) to see that this edition - whence the ink upon this page - saw starlight.

And lastly to Mike who has learned to walk tall - very tall.

I thank you one and all. God bless you.

- RFL

Dedication

To the Holy Spirit

Who reveals the Truth of Jesus - Savior Messiah - Son of God.
Thank you for showing me the WORD and the Word made FLESH.
AMEN!

"If incompletely I declare Thee… Blame not the art
But the Love I bare Thee"

Petrarch
Sonnets to Laura #54
circa 1338

Table of Contents

Page		
1		Introduction
5	1	God's Challenge
9	2	God's Time
13	3	The Feasts and Jesus
25	4	The 5 W's
35	5	God's Clock
41	6	Mysteries of the Moon
49	7	Anderson's Conversion Factor
53	8	Signs in the Heavens
53	A	Day of the Comet
60	B	Moon Struck
65	9	Stage 2000 - The Last Days
65	A	The Rebirth of Israel
75	B	Warning Flags
77	10	The Day and the Hour
87	11	When is the Rapture?
95	12	The Big Picture 430-480-430
105	13	The Big Picture as Prophecy
123	14	Segment Prophecy Block 480
123	A	A Year is a Day
125	B	David's Years
134	C	David's Days
136	D	Solomon's Days
143	15	Segment Prophecy Block 430
143	A	All Over Again
149	B	Meaning and Prophecy
153	16	God's Calculus
153	A	The Penalty Brick
155	B	Freewill Relations
157	C	Reject God = Death
163	D	7 Year Miracle
167	17	Promises, Promises
167	A	Days of Noah
180	B	The Days of the Sons

Appendices

183	I	Error Analysis
191	II	Giants in the Land
193	III	Jesus Denied/Baptist
197	IV	50 and 50 Again
201	V	Days in the Desert
203		Epilogue
205		A Note from the Author's Pastor

List of Illustrations

Figures

12	2-1	THE BIBLICAL LUNAR CALENDAR
13	3-1	THE FEASTS
17	3-2	JESUS AND THE FEASTS
46	6-1	EARTH - MOON ORBIT DIAGRAM
70	9A-1	CLEAN SLATE
96	12-1	430-480-430
97	12-2	THE TWO JUDGMENTS
100	12-3	430 X 3
122	13-1	GLORY TIMELINE
123	14A-1	A YEAR IS A DAY - OVERVIEW
125	14B-1	A YEAR IS A DAY - COMPRESSION
133	14B-2	THE PROPHECIES OF DAVID'S REIGN
139	14D-1	THE LAST DAYS
144	15A-1	FIRST JUBILEE
148	15A-2	SALVATION'S PROPHECY SPACE
157	16C-1	TEST BRICK
160	16C-2	KEY DATE BEFORE CRUCIFIXION
165	16D-1	7 YEAR MIRACLE
168	17-1	FLOOD SEGMENTS
176	17-2	DAYS OF NOAH; SEGMENT B: GIVING OF THE HOLY SPIRIT
177	17-3	DAYS OF NOAH; SEGMENT C
178	17-4	DAYS OF NOAH; THE LAST DAYS

Tables

Page	Table	Title
41	6-1	THE FLOOD YEARS
67	9A-1	PROPHECIES OF ISRAEL'S RETURN
73	9A-1	PROPHECIES OF ISRAEL'S RETURN (REPEATED)
115	13-1	COVENANT VIOLATIONS
134	14C-1	PLAGUES OF EGYPT
135	14C-2	PLAGUES OF EGYPT - VS - REVELATION
170	17-1	1500 PROPHETIC YEARS
171	17-2	PASSOVER TO FIRST FRUITS – 32 AD
179	17-3	THE THIRD DAY OF THE GLORY OF THE LORD
192	A2-1	SPIES OUT
195	A3-1	JESUS AND THE BAPTIST
198	A4-1	SPRING 1446 BC

INTRODUCTION

Have you ever sat down at your desk for a single purpose – just to get this one thing done – one ten minute job? But, the phone rings and your boss gives you a more immediate task to finish first. Then a co-worker knocks on your door and needs help with yet another small task...then the intercom buzzes and you're informed of an unannounced meeting in five minutes... and so goes the day. Before you know it, it took 10 hours to get your 10-minute task done. Life has a way of providing the unexpected in the most routine and recurring ways.

When I was a boy, my mother was given an expensive set of eight damask linen napkins. Mom was thrilled, but also chagrined; her dinnerware only had service for six. So dad, being a hero, bought her a jumbo set, complete with all the serving pieces, of fine bone china. But they only had knives and forks for six. So dad sprang for a complete set of Rogers Sterling Silverware in service for 8 – complete with all the serving pieces. Well, a place setting that elegant surely needed fine stemware and centerpieces and all the accouterments and together all this affluence needed a giant table (for 8 of course) to set upon and two giant cupboards – a breakfront with a credenza – to house all this tableware. Well, when this dining room *extraordinaire* was finally assembled, there wasn't a room in the house big enough to put it in! Thus, mom and dad bought a new house (and I got my own bedroom) all because of 8 fancy napkins.

Some things go like that. So it is with the story of Salvation. What started out as a three day journey, ended up taking over 3,000 years. One thing led to another and before you know it, 1446 BC is 1997 [AD!!] and we're still looking for heavenly help to get us out of this mess.

This story is real and it involves you and me. We are the first-string, front-line players in a game so one-sided that even Vegas wouldn't take the action. But, despite the predestined finish, we are stumbling around seemingly lost and done-in, stuck in the mud of sudden death; triple overtime no less. When will somebody score so we can pack up and go home? The answer is real easy. We can pack up and go home as soon as we learn to play by the rules and follow the Coach's instructions.

You see, God gave us this rulebook less than two months into the journey and told us how we were His number one handpicked team. We could have all the assistance we needed – even the occasional miracle – if we would just follow instructions and play by the rules. But we kept cheating or bragging or crying and God kept putting us in the penalty box and adding more periods (or innings or quarters) to the game – whatever was required to meet the offense. A little more playing time added here, a little more injury time added there, a bit of overtime for emphasis and thus here we are…………..1997 AD.

Every century or so, God would send in a super star prophet to help explain the rules and objectives of the game, but that didn't help. Every time we got close to the goal we would commit another major offense and end up further back than when we started. God can stretch out time the same way He stretched out space (to make the "playing field"). To God, time is a "thing" and He can pull some more out (like a magician pulling scarves out of his sleeve) any time He wants. Time is like a spy-glass telescope that has section after section being extended as far out as necessary for "seeing" better.

But for the most part, we, the players, just can't "see". The prophets could. They could see better than their counterparts and they gave loud and clear warnings about what was wrong with our game plan. The most amazing part of their message was the penalty phase – the time dilation/expansion/extension (or whatever) that pushed the finish line a little further out of reach.

This work is about those time extensions and the transcendent God that is "long suffering to this world" or as 2 Peter 3:8, 9 puts it:

> *"But do not forget this one thing dear friends: With the Lord a day is like a thousand years, and a thousand years are like a day. The Lord is not slow in keeping his promises, <u>as some understand slowness</u>. He is patient with you, not wanting anyone to perish, but everyone to come to repentance."*

In this work we will look at prophecy and outcomes that come true "precisely" – but in God's time. We will also look at events and judgments that have been determined and appointed [set in concrete], yet delayed again and again so that each of us might finally come to repentance. (Thank you, Jesus!)

The concept that 'sin promotes delay' (which we will examine in some detail) is a measure of unfathomable mercy and grace on God's part. We rebel and He delays [judgment]. We deserve punishment (death), but He extends mercy (otherwise no flesh would survive!) These "time delays", provided by grace alone, afford mankind the opportunity to meditate upon our rebellious nature, consider our rejection of God's mercy (Jesus), and thereby, some…….some………may come to repentance. These "delays by grace" may not be inexhaustible. When the sin of the Amorites "was full" God acted in judgment. And so it will be with all mankind……..and all too soon for some. Judgment or mercy…….your choice.

1.0 GOD'S CHALLENGE

There have been many attempts to set a date and time for the Second Advent - the return of our Savior Messiah - Jesus the Christ. Self-proclaimed prophets, leaders of radical Christian groups and plain old charlatans, have named the day and the hour for profit, scandal and notoriety. But...none have been proven correct.

Attempts to pre-announce the second coming of Jesus have been subject to ridicule by the secular world. Often this ridicule is subtly directed at the believing church rather than at the errant soothsayer. Literal interpretation of the Bible is mocked (everyone knows it's just a bunch of old fairy tales!!), the actions of devoted believers are scorned and, worst of all, the name of Jesus is debased. The Kingdom suffers loss.

But the Holy Scriptures (which this writer holds to be the inerrant Word of God) contain many end-times prophecies that seem to point to the world today as the last generation - the Last Days. Jewish and Christian scholars agree that we are approaching the end of the age. This being so, we had best be ready.

"*Wisdom* (we are told) *is justified of her children!*" (Matthew 11:19 KJV).

As the Western world approaches the end of the second millennium, we can expect numerous doomsday prophets to advertise and publish end of the world fantasies. Some level of superstitious fear will be manifest in our culture and certain authors, "psychics" and con men will make a small fortune off of our society's collective insecurity.

This is just one more voice among the many that claim to herald calamity or portend disaster. "BEWARE, THE SKY IS FALLING!!" But that is not the Christian message. Our gospel - the gospel of Jesus - is GOOD NEWS - joyous news - **the sky is falling** - Hooray - Hooray! Because that means Jesus is coming!! Nothing [absolutely nothing] could be better. (Praise God!).

I will examine time dependent prophecies and their precise fulfillment. There are many prophecies which operate as 'guidelines to the future.' They can only be interpreted properly when the precise nature of their temporal fulfillment is understood. They are of the highest value in unraveling the mystery of the "Time-line of Salvation." In Isaiah 41:22, God says:

> *"Bring in your idols to tell us what*
> *is going to happen...*
> *....Or declare to us the things to come, tell us*
> *what the future holds, so that we may know*
> *that you are gods."*

Thus the Creator of time challenges the forces of darkness which rule over our fallen world to demonstrate their "omniscience" - the transcendent all-knowingness which belongs to the nature of God alone. Again God says in Isaiah 42:9:

> *"...New things, I declare; before they spring into being, I announce*
> *them to you."*

[Jesus says to His disciples: *"See, I have told you ahead of time."* Matthew 24:25]

It seems quite clear. God is stating without reservation, that 'I alone can do this, I alone can transcend time. I alone can predict the future (it's Mine, after all, I made it!!)'! Again in Isaiah 44:7, God challenges the gods of this world to:

> *"Lay out before ME....*
> *What is yet to come....*
> *Foretell what will come!"*

God accepts His own challenge in Isaiah 46:9, 10. He states:

> *"I am God, and there is no other;*
> *I am God, and there is none like me.*
> *I <u>make known</u> the end from the beginning,*
> *from ancient times, what is still to come.*
> *I say: My purpose will stand, and*
> *I will do all that I please."*

The Lord Himself uses the fulfillment of prophecy as **proof** of His being and nature. We, therefore, should approach this subject with all due reverence. It is declared to be Holy.

The Scriptures reveal God's "plan" of salvation for man. Like any "plan", it has a beginning and an end. It has objectives to be gained and strategies to be employed and it has a precise time-line of execution. God stakes His reputation (the Greatness of His Holy Name) on the precision of His time-line. Along that time-line there is no greater event in all history than the return of Jesus Christ...... in GLORY!

The prophecy of Daniel 9:25 ff, pin-points the first advent of the Lamb of God precisely - to the very day!! Is there no similar prophecy for the exact time of His second advent - an even greater event?

Western theology has treated this subject with justifiable awe - bordering on superstition. If God boldly asserts that His NAME and His character can be found in the prophecies, why would the timing of the greatest event in salvation history be hidden from view? When the ultimate purpose of creation's existence (and our existence) is to give glory to God and when the purpose of the Scriptures is to reveal and glorify Jesus *("In the volume of the Book it is written of me"* Psalm 40:7 KJV). Why would the timing of the ultimate shining glory be veiled?

Perhaps it is not!

God says: *"I make known the end from the beginning."*

Perhaps through the working of the Holy Spirit, we can rightly divide the Word....and the answer has been there all along.

2.0 TIME

Because God created time, it is His to use as it pleases Him. Time is the 'stage' on which the plan of salvation - the Passion play - unfolds. Time is so precious an indicator, that God gave to the Jews (and to all believers) a separate (and therefore Holy) way of measuring and tracking time. The Sun and the Moon were created for that purpose.

> *"And God said, Let there be lights in the firmament of the heaven to divide the day from the night; and let them be for signs, and for seasons, and for days, and years: And let them be for lights in the firmament of the heaven to give light upon the earth: and it was so.*
>
> *And God made two great lights; the greater light to rule the day, and the lesser light to rule the night: he made the stars also. And God set them in the firmament of the heaven to give light upon the earth, and to rule over the day and over the night, and to divide the light from the darkness: and God saw that it was good. And the evening and the morning were the fourth day."* (Genesis 1:14-19 KJV)

In verse 15, the Word says the first purpose of these celestial objects was...."*to give light to the earth.*" Thanks be to God that we can all enjoy the warmth and beauty of a sunny day or the peacefulness of a moon-lit night. Physically, these objects have done God's purpose but is there deeper revelation? Does the phrase "to give light to the earth" have a spiritual aspect as well?

Light was the fourth property of creation.

In the beginning (time), *God created the Heavens* (space) *and the Earth* (matter). *And then God said: "Let there be light."* (energy)

From modern physics, we know that space and time and matter are all manifestations of oneness. They exist together in a point called "singularity". Light spans this creation-space and defines the limits of action within the space. E =

mc²]

That's all well and good for Einstein and fans of relativistic mechanics - but isn't it strange that a bunch of ignorant nomadic herdsmen, wandering 40 years (lost in the desert!), should state the fundamental properties of the universe's design so clearly in the first three verses of their "folklore"?

More seriously - we know God is light, truth is light, that the people living in darkness have seen a great light, and that that light was the light of men.

The Holy Spirit calling attention to the light of the Sun and Moon - days and years - gives us reason to consider whether such 'light' would be used to give glory to Jesus (of course!!!) Yes, of course it does! Even the calendar praises God!!

On the seventh day, God called the work of creation "very good." God gave us a calendar based on the works of creation (the Sun and Moon). Thus we might suspect such a calendar to be "very good" as well.

In this work, we will use the Sun and Moon and the length of the original day and month when calculating and computing solutions for time-based prophecy. The length of our day (today) is significantly different from that of Adam and Eve's and our month is also different. When we use the original clock God instituted at creation [and told us to use], the results obtained in prophecy determinations are both astounding and convergent.

The lunar clock is based on the cycle of the Moon in it's orbiting of the Earth. Each revolution (or one cycle or period) takes 29.53 days. But the lunar period was not always 29.53 days. Once upon a time, it was 30 days exactly.

The reasons for the difference between the 30-day period at creation and the 29.53 day cycle today will be discussed in Chapter 8.

The lunar year had 12 months of 30 days each, or 360 days per year. Today, the lunar year is still 12 months, but only 354 days (29.5 x 12). Some lunar months have 30 days, some lunar months have 29 days - but each standard lunar year has 354 days. That's 11, and sometimes 12 (leap-year) days per year less than our solar (sun-based) calendar. Julius Caesar developed our solar calendar so that he could have "military precision" in the operation of the supply lines and tactics used by the Roman Legions. There were some flaws in this "Julian" calendar that became obvious over centuries.

Pope Gregory fixed some of the problems in 1584 and gave us the Gregorian Calendar. This celestial schedule still has problems but they are only obvious over millennia.

Do you ever wonder why Easter is on a different Sunday each year? Sometimes early and sometimes late? That is because Easter depends, in part, on the lunar calendar. The lunar calendar, with 354 days per year, gets out of phase with the solar calendar very quickly. Every year or two, an extra lunar month (a leap month called 'second Adar') is added to realign the two systems. Virtually all primitive societies used some form of a lunar - based calendar. The Mayan culture's lunar calendar implementation is possibly the most famous. But for our purposes we will use the Jewish lunar calendar given by God in the Bible. God chose to use the New Moon just after the Spring Equinox (March 21 - 1st day of Spring) as the start of the year. A "new moon" is defined as that time when the first sliver of the white of the Moon (after having been all black) is seen from Jerusalem. The 1st of each month is defined by each successive "new moon". "New moon" days were festival days in Israel. The enemies of Israel even tried announcing a new moon "unofficially" to the more remote parts of Israel to confuse military orders and religious worship services! The 'new moon' had to be seen with the human eye - not calculated. Cloudy nights could cause <u>BIG</u> problems. The official announcement of "new moon" always came from the priests who ran the Temple!

The differences between the lunar calendar and the solar calendar are so great that it takes a sophisticated computer program to align the two calendar systems accurately. Knowing when a "new moon" was seen over Jerusalem by a sentry in King David's army is a hard element to determine. Exactly when the ancients chose to insert an extra month in the lunar year is also a bit subjective. Over time, the Temple priests developed standing rules for these procedures. For work in this text, by-hand estimates for conversion between lunar and solar calendars are used. We will not need space-flight accuracy. Where improved accuracy might help clarify things, the reader is encouraged to try his hand at precise conversions.

The lunar calendar used by Abraham and Moses and Jesus, appears in Figure 2-1.

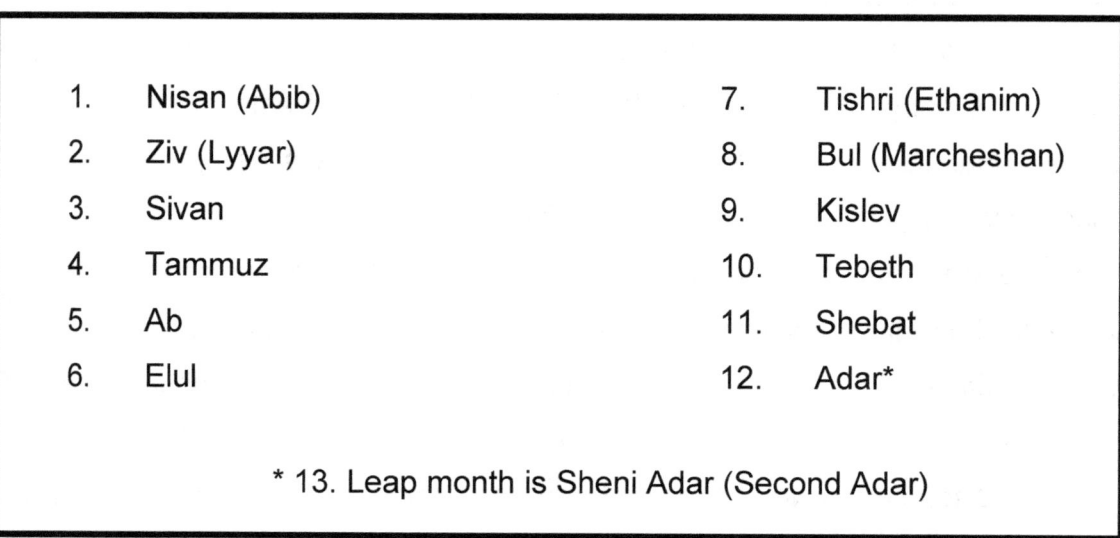

1.	Nisan (Abib)	7.	Tishri (Ethanim)
2.	Ziv (Lyyar)	8.	Bul (Marcheshan)
3.	Sivan	9.	Kislev
4.	Tammuz	10.	Tebeth
5.	Ab	11.	Shebat
6.	Elul	12.	Adar*

* 13. Leap month is Sheni Adar (Second Adar)

Figure 2-1
THE BIBLICAL LUNAR CALENDAR

[NOTE: There are actually two major Jewish lunar calendars. The religious calendar used by the priests for holidays and feasts, and the civil calendar used by the government which is exactly 6 months out of phase with the priest's religious calendar. This is similar to the way the U.S. Government has a "fiscal year" starting on October 1st, and a standard calendar using January 1st for the start of a new year. There are other Jewish lunar calendars which historians must struggle with such as the calendar for agricultural events (and Tithing), but they do not affect our work here. All lunar events in this work use the Religious Calendar shown in Figure 2.1.]

3.0 THE FEASTS AND JESUS

In Leviticus 23, God institutes seven feasts for His glory. These seven High Holy days [and they certainly should be considered High Holy days seeing as how they were hand-picked by God Himself!] are major predictors and milestones in God's plan of salvation. These feasts are shown in Figure 3.1.

	English	Hebrew	Time
Spring	1. Passover	Pesach	14th of Nisan
	2. Unleavened Bread	Hag Ha Matzah	15th of Nisan
	3. First Fruits	*Bikkurim	Day after 1st regular Sabbath of Hag Ha Matzah
	4. Pentecost	Shavout	First Fruits plus 50 days
Fall	5. Trumpets	Yom Teruah	1st of Tishri
	6. Atonement	Yom Kippur	10th of Tishri
	7. In-Gathering	Sukkot	15th -21st of Tishri

*This day does not have a unique name in Jewish tradition, but is referred to as 'the offering of the First Fruits'. "Bikkurim" is my literal substitution for the term "First Fruits".

Figure 3-1

THE FEASTS

The Feasts are divided into two groups, the first four are in the Spring and the last three are in the Fall.

As Joseph Good points out in his work on Rosh HaShanah [1], the two groups of Feasts are in fact the "Former Rains" and the "Latter Rains" of which Hosea 6:3 speaks:

---

[1] *Rosh HaShanah and the Messianic Kingdom to Come*, Joseph Good, 1989, Hatikva Ministries, Pt. Arthur, Tx.

"....and He (the Lord) shall come unto us as the rain,
as the latter and former rain unto the earth." (KJV)

Therefore, when taken in their fullest Messianic meaning, the Feasts illustrate the first and second comings of Jesus. Thus the Feasts are special prophetic days and celebrate major events in God's dealings with the Jews (the chosen People - chosen to make God's name great - i.e., chosen for service to glorify God). These special days also reflect major events in the agricultural year (harvesting) and most importantly these days represent events (both past (former rains) and future (latter rains)) in the revelation of the glory of the Messiah Christ Jesus.

From our readings of the Old and New Testaments, we are familiar with the deep Messianic significance of the first four Feasts:

1. <u>Passover:</u>   THE BLOOD OF THE LAMB!

The only protection from the Angel of Death was to hide under the Blood. From the first sin in the Garden of Eden to Abraham's faith in YHWH, a lamb has been the <u>substitute</u> slain for man's sin. At the first Passover, God instituted criteria and procedures for this symbolic ceremony. The lamb had to be spotless - without blemish - perfect in every way. What lamb is so perfect, we should ask - behold the Lamb of God... (John 1:29).

On the 10th of the month (of Nisan), the believing Jew would take that lamb into <u>his house</u> to be examined and known by the whole family. It was on the 10th of Nisan that God's lamb, Jesus, entered <u>God's house</u>, the Temple in Jerusalem, to be examined and tested by the scribes and the Pharisees so that they might know Him whom they would slay. On the 14th of Nisan, the chosen sacrificial lamb was taken by the High Priest and tied to the Temple altar at 9 AM - so also Jesus was taken and tied (nailed) to the tree - the Tree of Life - the Cross - at 9 AM. And at 3 PM precisely, the High Priest cut the lamb's throat saying, "It is finished!" (Meaning: The sacrifice has been offered.) At 3 PM, Jesus, the Lamb of God, also declared that "It is finished" and surrendered His life...a ransom for many.

Since Christ was crucified from the foundation of the world, God, in His passion that everyone "might kiss the Son" (Psalm 2), built into the original Passover special elements, all of the pointers and all of the signs necessary to see the mystery of Messiah fulfilled in Christ Jesus.

But why was the timing of the events of Passover so perfect and precise? Couldn't Jesus have died at any time on any day and still be the one and only acceptable sacrifice? Yes, of course!! But in instituting the Festivals, God was setting up the Passion play and commanding that man <u>rehearse</u> the lines and scenes from the play precisely for 1500 prophetic years. [Note: 1500 prophetic years is 1478 calendar years (1500A = 1478) starting from 1446 BC and counting 1478 Passovers gives us the year 32 AD the cross of Jesus.] In this way, every ingredient and every nuance of the substitutional ceremony would be known and available for meditation. You see, God said, "Last of all I will send my own Son - surely they will honor Him." Matthew 21:37 (paraphrased).

[Jesus' words, "Father forgive them for they <u>know not</u> what they do," has even greater significance when you consider the irony that after 1500 rehearsals, they still <u>did</u> <u>not know</u> what they were doing].

That is why the coincident timing of the events is of such major significance. When God instituted His feast, He required that all Jewish men be present in Jerusalem at the "appointed time." A Hebrew term for feast is "Mo'ed" which means "set-time." (See J. Good, Rosh HaShanah, Chapter 3).

The exact time for the Lamb of God to redeem the world through blood sacrifice was "set" from eternity. All Jewish men were to be there to bare witness to God's mercy.

- *See I will declare a work to you before hand.* (Fulfilled John 14:29)
- *...Abraham rejoiced at the thought of seeing my day;* ***and he saw it****.* (John 8:56)

There on the mountains of Moriah - the same mountain that Jesus would die on - in perfect obedience - there Abraham, in his act of obedience, saw in a vision the lamb that God would provide. (Genesis 22:13)

The Lord declares that these times are "set" (Mo'ed) - "appointed" from eternity and they will come to pass. **Precisely on schedule**.

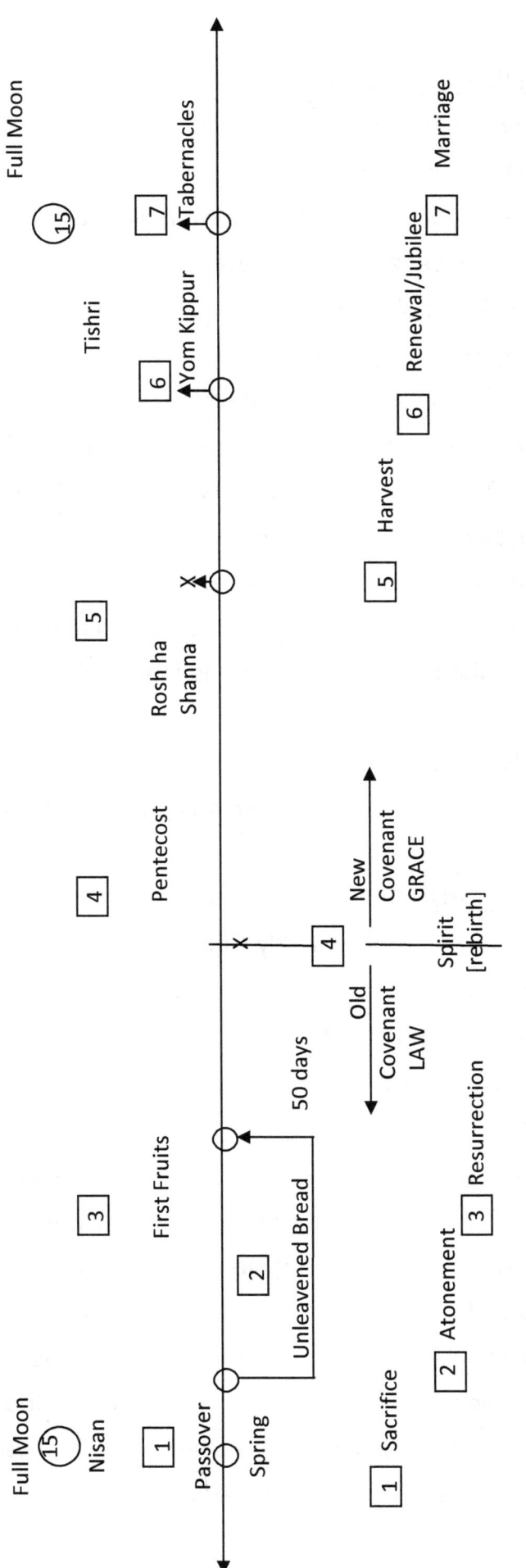

Figure 3-2

JESUS AND THE FEASTS

2.   UNLEAVENED BREAD:

After the Passover of 1446 BC, the Jews were given permission to go and worship their God - to leave Egypt, the land of slavery (to sin) behind - to be separated from the world for the purpose of worship - to glorify God.

Our desire to be separated - to leave the world and sin behind - should be equally as intense. There should be no time spent letting bread rise - the time to leave is now. <u>Today</u> is the day of Salvation!

Paul says in I Corinthians 5:8: *"Therefore let us <u>keep the feast</u> not with old leaven...but with the unleavened bread of sincerity and truth."*

Why would Paul encourage this Christian church to "keep the feast"? Isn't this a Jewish holiday? **NO! It's God's holiday!** - one of seven - instituted to show believers the deepest meaning of Messiah.

As believers, we are also called to be separated and to eat the unleavened bread - the bread of life - the true Manna. (See John 6:35 - *"I am the bread of life."*)

We, the Redeemed, should also partake of this festival and celebrate before the whole world the mercy that God has given us to feast on.

3.   FIRST FRUITS:

The first Sunday after the weekly Sabbath of Passover week ("Passover") is the Festival of First Fruits, the beginning of the spring barley harvest. Jesus begins that harvest by His rising from the dead. *("And the graves were opened; and many bodies of the saints which slept arose." Matthew 27:52 KJV)* Death was left behind in an empty tomb.

The initial celebration of first fruits (from the dead) was a major milestone in Jewish history. The Jews were resurrected from a watery grave 3 days after the original Passover. Two million frightened souls stood on the shores of the Red Sea terrified of Pharaoh and his on-rushing army. But these beleaguered refugees saw that the way to freedom provided by God was through the Valley of Death. Down they went into the Red Sea, protected by God on all sides. They emerged - resurrected from death - on the other side. They were the first fruits of salvation. When the grave closed over the unbelievers and swallowed them in defeat, the Jews were then physically free of Egypt. (Prior to his death Pharaoh still owned them. Now they belonged to God!) Satan was defeated, Death was defeated, and it was on to the Promised Land. (God's next gift would be Jesus and rest, but more on this later.)

4. PENTECOST:

From the first fruits of a new life out of Egypt and freedom from Pharaoh, the Jews proceed 50 days to Mount Sinai to meet with God - to hear His voice and to receive His rulebook - the Law. This was the first Pentecost or Feast of Weeks. The "set" appointment for Pentecost was prophetically fulfilled in the upper room when the Holy Ghost, the Spirit of God, descended on the first church. With the Spirit of Jesus in their hearts (Acts 4:33), the Apostles were ready to do the work for which they had been both chosen and separated - to glorify God and His work in the Messiah Christ Jesus.

All of the spring feasts (the former rain) were fulfilled by Messiah at His first coming. None of the first four feasts instituted by God were random or whimsical events. They were uniquely specified and ordained by **historic events** in Jewish nationhood and were to be celebrated by the precise observance of the lunar calendar. Yes, the feasts are historic events, but they are also prophetic symbols.

The actual fulfillment of these prophetic symbols takes place in the life and work of the Messiah. This work will show that other **historic events** were precise prophecy of future feast fulfillments. These events in the life of Jesus are shown in Figure 3-2.

God shaped all of pre-salvation history with events and milestones - road markers and neon signs - proclaiming the glory of the coming Messiah His Son. What father wouldn't advertise his son's grand performance of righteousness?

So God ordained and orchestrated celebrations, festivals and precise rituals which pointed to and proclaimed the work of Messiah. But like any grand festival, history required a precise schedule - so that all righteousness might be fulfilled at the precise appointed (Mo'ed) time. God says His Word is good and dependable - we can count on it! How can we count on it if the schedule is arbitrary or unknown? **How can we be in Jerusalem** at the appointed time if we don't have a schedule and a clock?

Well, fret not! - God has given us the schedule for the future in His prophecy and feasts. That schedule uses the same clock as the original plan - the cycle of the Moon! The major events left to be fulfilled by, in, and through Messiah Jesus are the Fall Feasts - the Latter Rain - satisfied and accomplished at the second coming. These unfulfilled feasts are:

5. Trumpets
6. Atonement
7. In-Gathering (Tabernacles)

These feasts, the last of the seven ordained by God, all occur in the seventh month of the religious year, the month of Tishri.

5. TRUMPETS - YOM TERUAH:

Leviticus 23 has little to say about the feast of Trumpets. We are simply told that the first day of the seventh month is a Holy day of rest - blow the trumpet (Shofar). What is the purpose of this day? God has left us important clues in His Word. The Scripture is filled with prophetic references to the blowing of the trumpet. These God-ordained uses of the trumpet blast are to: alert, alarm, announce, proclaim and assemble the children of Israel.

There are two types of trumpets described in Scripture: silver trumpets (2) and the ram's horn (Shofar). God ordained the two silver trumpets to be used to maintain order and discipline when the Jews were crossing the desert. The silver trumpets were sounded to order the line of march and they were also sounded to call the leaders (or all the people) to an assembly. These same two silver trumpets were used to call the people to war (especially to remind warriors that the battle belonged to the Lord!). Lastly, these two silver trumpets were used to announce the festivals ordained by God.

The other trumpet ordained by God is the ram's horn - the Shofar. It is blown on two occasions: on the Feast of Trumpets and to proclaim Jubilee.

From the lunar calendar (see Figure 2-1), we see that the seventh month is called "Tishri". This is also the first month of the civil calendar. Therefore, the first of Tishri is both Yom Teruah (the Day of Trumpets) and Rosh HaShanah (New Year's Day). The blowing of the trumpet reminds us that God will bring judgment on His enemies on this day, Yom haDin, the day of judgment, sounding the Heavenly Shofar Himself! (See Zechariah 9:14 ff) This period of judgment begins on the 1st of Tishri and continues for nine more days. On the 10th of Tishri, God offers atonement for sinners who have repented during this period. The 10th of Tishri is called Yom Kippur (the Day of Atonement). The ten-day period, from the 1st of Tishri to the 10th of Tishri, is known as "the days of awe" (Yamin Nora`im).

These ten days will play an important part in the prophecy fulfillments we will examine in the coming chapters. Remember, these are pre-selected days that God designed to illustrate Jesus - and to give glory to the Son of God.

The Shofar, or Ram's horn, is also used by God to announce the start of Jubilee Year. A Jubilee Year is to be celebrated every 50 years. It is a Sabbath year. The most distinguishing feature of the Jubilee Year is summed up in the word "RETURN." The wandering people are to return to and be reunited with their ancestral clans and families. Freedom is to be returned to the captives, debts are to be forgiven and all land is to be returned to it's original owners within the clan or family inheritance. This process achieves "restoration", as all things are returned to their original initial condition - restored - made new *("Behold, all things are become new." 2 Corinthians 5:17 KJV)*.

The Jubilee Year begins at sundown with the blowing of the Shofar on the Day of Atonement, Yom Kippur, the 10th of Tishri, the seventh month.

6. <u>ATONEMENT - Yom Kippur:</u>

Yom Kippur is the most solemn of the Jewish High Holy days instituted by God. It is a day God says "to deny yourselves". It was on this one day a year that the High Priest entered into the Most Holy Place, The Holy of Holies, offering to God the blood of a sacrificial goat used as a symbol of atonement - a blood covering - for the sins of the Nation Israel.

The Book of Hebrews describes the role of Messiah Jesus as He offers His own blood in the Heavenly Tabernacle - once for all! An act that never needs repeating, for the blood of Jesus cleanses all believers, past, present and future, from their impurity.

With the perfect [efficacious] atonement having already been made in Heaven for us by Jesus, it seems as though this God-ordained festival has already been satisfied. What action would be left for Jesus to do (on earth) on Yom Kippur now that He has achieved eternal reconciliation for His church?

Well, what did Jesus do immediately after the eternal atonement? The Scripture reads (Hebrews 10:12-13):

> *"...he sat down at the right hand of God. Since that time he <u>waits</u> for his enemies to be made his footstool."*

Yom Kippur is also called Yom haDin - day of Judgment [the last of the 10 "Days of Awe"]. Jesus, sitting at the right hand of God, is in the judgment position. He waits for the appointed time ("Mo`ed) for God's wrath to fall on the unbelievers, the unrepentant.

Repentance means everything to God. Repentance is a process of 'cleansing unto God'. When repentance is present in a person, that soul is without pride, humble before God and openly confessing the sinful errors of a past life. When repentance is **not** present in a person, they are hard-hearted, filled with pride and unbelieving in God, wrath or judgment. In this work we will examine instances of repentance and their effect on history. God is so moved by repentance that He will even change '**time**' in order to provide an opportunity for repentance.

The Jews honored God with a 40-day period of repentance. This period of repentance is called "TESHUVAH". This soul cleansing period begins on the 1st day of the sixth month, Elul, and continues through the 10th of Tishri – Yom Kippur. These forty days will play a major role in the history of Israel. These events are foreshadowed via the prophetic life of King David as imagery of Jesus and the last days. A detailed explanation of this imagery and foreshadowing of David as a type of Christ is provided in Chapter 15.

7. IN-GATHERING (TABERNACLES OR SUKKOT):

The last fall feast, Tabernacles, is the most joyous of all the Jewish feasts. It not only celebrates the in-gathering of the fall harvest, but also God's dwelling with His people.

Tabernacles celebrates those days in the desert when the Glory of the Lord visited and rested on the nation of Israel. With God among them, they had need of nothing. He gave them water in the desert, bread from heaven and quail at sunset. Their shoes didn't wear out and their clothes didn't fray. They were on their way to the Promised Land and God was leading them.

What could be better?

Here we have a glorious picture of the Messianic Kingdom - the Millennium - the 1,000 years of peace with Jesus leading (ruling) His chosen people.

If this is also a Jubilee year - then all rightful things are returned and put in their proper place, i.e. restored! (And as we will see Jesus will return in a Jubilee year!!!!!!)

We will celebrate in a restored world!!! The curse is put away, Satan is bound, and we can sit at the feet of Jesus. ("...*They will neither harm nor destroy on all my Holy mountain*" Isaiah 65:25.)

This will be the time for Jesus to assume His rightful place as King - [which requires a coronation] and to celebrate His marriage with the Bride (the church) [which requires a wedding feast].

It is interesting to note that in a Jubilee year, in the month of Tishri, seven trumpets sound. Two trumpets sound to announce Rosh HaShanah; two trumpets sound to proclaim Yom Kippur; and the Shofar Ha Gadol (the Great Trumpet) marks sunset of Yom Kippur, the start of the Jubilee. Trumpets 6 and 7 announce the celebration of Tabernacles - God with us!. The sounding of seven trumpets is also a very solemn reminder of the seven trumpets of Judgment and wrath found in The Book of the Revelation. Which trumpets will you hear? The seven for wrath or the seven for celebration?

It is also interesting to speculate that Sukkot (Tabernacles) might be the birthday of Jesus. The one requirement of the millennium is that all nations must come before the King on this day. (See Zechariah 14:16ff)

Jesus' birthday may be estimated from clues found in Scripture.

Zechariah, the father of John the Baptist, was a priest of the division of Abijah. I Chronicles 24:10 tells us that the 'eighth lot' or period of Temple service fell to the family of Abijah. The eighth <u>regular</u> service period is the 10th week of the year (week #3 Passover and week #9 Pentecost, have <u>special</u> service). It was during his regular Temple service that Zechariah was told he would have a son. So sometime after week 10 ends - according to Elizabeth's fertility cycle, John the Baptist was conceived - sometime around week 12, or 3 months into 5 BC. John's birth occurred 9 months later. Since 3 months plus 9 months equals 12 months - John's birth was in the first month - about Passover- of 4 BC. Jesus was born six months after that (via Luke 1:26). Passover is in Nisan the first month - so six months later is the seventh month, Tishri - the Feast of Tabernacles. The infant Jesus was born in a "stable" - **<u>a booth - Sukkah</u>** (singular) during the Feast of Sukkot (plural) because there was no room at the inn. Why? Because the City of Jerusalem and all the inns of the surrounding countryside (including Bethlehem) were full of pilgrims celebrating the festival(s) of Tabernacles.

> [Note: Luke tells us that Joseph went to Bethlehem to register for the census (Luke 2:4,5). This is surely true. But what we also see is a very devout man taking his family to worship God at the feast of Tabernacles (in Jerusalem) and a very practical man registering for the census (in Bethlehem) during the same pilgrimage!]

4.0 The Five W's

Acts 18:28 tells us that Appollos would publicly refute the Jews:
"*In proving from the Scriptures that Jesus was the Christ.*"

Can you do that? Prove by the Scriptures that Jesus was the Messiah - using only the Old Testament? (That's all Appollos had! Paul and Peter and John hadn't written the New Testament yet. It was in their hearts, but not yet in their heads!) I've often wondered what Appollos might have used as evidence - which references, which prophecies? Who knows, for there is plenty to choose from. "...In the volume of the book it is written of me." (Psalm 40:7) But sadly, the average Christian does not understand or appreciate Jewish Messianic expectations. Alfred Edersheim, in his tome "*The Life and Times of Jesus the Messiah*", gives a remarkable portrait of first century Rabbinic thought concerning Israel's attitudes and aspirations for the Anointed One of God. (Book II, Chapter 5). Appendix IX contains a list of Messianically applied OT passages found in ancient Rabbinic writings. Edersheim conveys Jewish Messianic expectations of the first century with remarkable insight and clarity. The New Testament teaches that Jesus is the Alpha and the Omega, the beginning and the end. In other words Jesus is all in all. Edersheim shows that Rabbinic teachings of Messiah also included everything in between Alpha and Omega. The following examples from Sanhedrin writings are classic illustrations of the all-in-all nature of Rabbinic Messiah.

All the prophets prophesied not
But of the day of Messiah   *(1) Sanh 99A*

The world was not created
But only for the Messiah   *(2) Sanh 98b*

To the devout Jew and Rabbinic teacher the Messiah was **everything** - as these passages clearly show. There are over 450 specific prophecies concerning Messiah cited by Edersheim and his list is not exhaustive! Only those scripture references are listed for which there are extant ancient Rabbinic commentaries. With so much to glean from it should be easy to show that the "Anointed One" so eagerly anticipated by Israel was in fact Jesus of Nazareth. Because this text deals with the precise fulfillment of the Word of God, we will only cite references here that illustrate this level of precision. (Prophecy that is more objective than subjective.)

Let's try to fill out the standard reporter's questionnaire or prosecutor's trial matrix. Let's answer the five W's: the Who, What, When, Where and Why (and we'll throw in "how" as well), and see if we can find enough evidence "to convict Jesus of being the Messiah."

Were the following references indicative of Jesus of Nazareth or did they reference some other missed and long forgotten pretender?

- Son of God
- Son of Man
- High Priest
- Prophet
- King of Israel
- Lamb of God
- Messiah
- Anointed One

Who did Jesus say he was? What did the prophets have to say about this coming One?

Let's take a look.

[**WHO**] is this "Messiah" or "Anointed One"?

1. Isaiah 7:14

Therefore the Lord himself will give you a sign: the Virgin will be with child and will give birth to a son, and will call him Immanuel.

Theologians can argue the virgin birth until they are blue in the face but in reality, could the conception of God Himself have happened in the physical? What do you mean "God Himself?" you may ask? - Note the association of the child as "Immanuel", in other words as "God with us". The conception of this child, who is God, must therefore be spiritually achieved and not physically achieved (man cannot create God).

2. Genesis 49:10:

The scepter will not depart from Judah nor the ruler's staff from between his feet until he comes to whom it (tribute) belongs and the obedience of nations is his.

We look for this 'child' to be a King - the King of all nations - born of the Tribe of Judah.

3. Isaiah 9:6ff

For to us a child is born, To us a son is given and the government will be on his shoulder. And he will be called Wonderful Counselor, Mighty God, Everlasting Father, Prince of Peace. Of the increase of his government and peace there will be no end. He will reign on David's throne and over his kingdom...

This male child will be called God - He will be king over 'Israel', and a member of the house of David. How do we know He is from the house of David?

Isaiah 11:1, 2a

A shoot will come up from the stump of Jesse; from his roots a Branch will bear fruit. The Spirit of the Lord will rest on Him...

The Jesse that Isaiah was referring to was the father of David - so one from David's line will be called the Branch.

[**WHAT**] is this "Messiah" or "Anointed One"?

1. Psalm 2:6-7

I have installed my King

On Zion, my Holy hill.

I will proclaim the degree of the Lord:

He said to me, "You are my Son;

Today I have become your father.

What is this child of the house of David but **God's own Son**! (And King of

Israel).

> 2. Psalm 110:4
>
> *The Lord has sworn and will not change his mind: "You are a <u>priest</u> forever in the Order of Melchizedek."*

What is this child - both King **and** priest?

[WHEN] will this Messiah come?

> Daniel 9:25
>
> <u>Know and understand this:</u>
>
> *From the issuing of the decree to restore and rebuild Jerusalem until the Anointed One, the ruler, comes, there will be 7 sevens and 62 sevens (483 prophetic years)*
>
> *....the Anointed One will be cut off* (killed).

As will be shown in Chapter 5, 483 prophetic years is 476 regular years and this period ends in 32 AD - when Jesus is crucified (cut off).

[WHERE] will the Messiah come?

> 1. WHERE TO BE BORN
>
> Micah 5:2
>
> *But you, Bethlehem <u>Ephrathah,</u> though you are small among the clans of Judah, out of you will come for me one who will be ruler over Israel, whose origins are from of old - from ancient times.*

So our child - Eternal Son of God - priest and king will be born in Bethlehem. But which Bethlehem (House of Bread) - there are several such places. Note: <u>Ephrathah</u> - not just the town (Bethlehem) is named but also the ancient name for the township or area (Ephrathah) so that there is no mistaking which village is meant. This is the Bethlehem just outside Jerusalem, where the lambs for temple sacrifice are penned.

> 2. WHERE TO DIE:
>
> Zechariah 9:9
>
> *Rejoice greatly, O Daughter of Zion! Shout Daughter of Jerusalem! See, your king comes to you, righteous and having*

> *salvation, gentle and riding on a donkey, on a colt, the foal of a donkey.*

This king will come to Jerusalem bringing the people "salvation."

[WHY] does Messiah Die:

1. Genesis 3:15 (KJV)   [God addressing Satan]

   I will put enmity between thee and the woman, and between thy seed and her seed; It (Messiah) shall bruise thy head, and thou shalt bruise his heel.

God promises Satan that he will pay for what he has done. The blood of Messiah will set free the prisoners of Satan (sin).

2. Exodus 6:6-7

   I will free you...

   I will redeem you with an outstretched arm...

   I am the Lord

How much more 'outstretched' can one's arm get than to be crucified?

3. Isaiah 53:8

   ...For he was cut-off from the land of the living;

   For the transgressions of my people he was stricken.

4. Isaiah 53:5

   ...He was crushed for our iniquities; The punishment that brought us peace was upon Him, and by His wounds we are healed.

God Himself will do this work of redeeming and setting free - He is the One who saves.

5. Isaiah 53:6

   The Lord has laid on him the iniquity of us all.

Jesus died to take our punishment on Himself. The price of our sin has been paid.

6. Isaiah 53:10

   Yet it was the Lord's will to crush him and cause Him to suffer...

   the Lord makes His life a guilt offering.

God made Jesus, His own son, our atonement!

Are you sure this Messiah's name is Jesus?
[WHO]
1. Zechariah 6:12

Tell him this is what the Lord Almighty says: "Here is the man whose name is THE BRANCH."

The person God was talking about had the same name as the Messiah! To whom was the Lord speaking? To the High Priest, Jeshua - (Jesus - he who saves) and 6:13 tells us He will also wear a King's crown - King and priest in one.

[HOW] will the Messiah Jeshua Die?
1. Psalm 22:7, 8, 14, 16, 17 & 18

All who seek me mock at me
They hurl insults, shaking their heads:
He trusts in the Lord; let the Lord rescue Him.
I am poured out like water, and all my bones are out of joint.
My heart has turned to wax; It has melted away within me.
....they have pierced my hands and my feet
I can count all my bones;
People stare and gloat over me.
They divide my garments among them
and cast lots for my clothing.

How was Jeshua, Son of God, King and High Priest, cut off - He was pierced in His hands and feet. He was crucified!

2. Isaiah 53:5a

But he was pierced for _____'s transgressions. [put your own name in the blank!]

3. Zechariah 12:10 c, d

...They will look on me, the one they have pierced, and they will mourn for him as one mourns for an only child...a first-born son.

When those who crucified God's only Son see Him at the Second Coming, they will understand - and grieve and mourn!

There are hundreds of other scriptures which point clearly to Jesus and His ministry and His sacrifice. Anyone willing to look (and see) will find that it is true: "In the volume of the Book it is written of me"! (Psalm 40:7)(Praise God!!).

[Note: A similar and probably more masterful rendition of the detective's matrix can be found in Josh McDowell's: <u>Evidence That Demands A Verdict</u> (©Copyright Campus Crusade for Christ, Inc. 1972,1979.)]

<u>God's Master Plan</u>:

With the approach of the year 2000 AD Christianity will begin it's third millennium. But "creation" will be ending its sixth millennium. There are several ways to arrive at this conclusion. In 1654, James Ussher, the Arch Bishop of Armagh in Ireland, published his documented dating of creation, <u>Annals Yeteris et Novi Testamentio.</u> Ussher assigned a creation date of 4004BC. He arrived at this date using the ages of the patriarch's at fatherhood given in the Scriptures (Genesis 5). Beginning at Adam's begetting Seth (when Adam was 130 years old), and continuing up to Joseph and the period of slavery in Egypt, Ussher summed the period of Genesis. He then chronicled from Moses through Judges, to reach the reign of David. Then Ussher traced the annals of the kings of the House of Judah up to Zedekiah the last King of the house of Judah, to find the years to the fall of Jerusalem (586 BC). From there, he added the period of captivity in Babylon to the history of the building of the Second Temple and tied these records to the ancient records of the Persian kings to get Nehemiah's return during the twentieth year of King Artaxerxes. From there, he was able to align events with the records of ancient Greece (which fought major wars with the Persians) to make a continuum of Israel's history for measurement and critique.

Using this technique, Ussher arrived at a date of 4004 BC for the Creation. Anyone who has attempted to build a time line of the Old Testament, or has otherwise engaged an Old Testament chronology, knows how difficult the bishop's task was. Following Ussher's approach, I have personally built such a time line up to the Second Temple with extra-Biblical linkage to King Artaxerxes.

[Note: A missionary brother of mine, Mr. John Moore of Cedar Crest, NM, has continued this time-line to the Crucifixion. The task is especially difficult because the record is not simplistically continuous but rather builtby logical inference and deduction from small scraps of truth scattered innocuously through-out both the Old and New Testaments. I am indebted to Mr. Moore for his diligence and perseverance on the project.]

Building a trustworthy chronology up to the reign of the Persian Monarch Artaxerxes is quite important because events in the twentieth year of Artaxerxes' reign are paramount to fixing the starting point of Daniel's prophecy of the advent and death of the Messiah Jesus and to the prophesy of the end of the age - Daniel's 70th week. This prophecy is explained in more detail in Chapter 5.

The dating of creation by James Ussher at 4004 BC appears in general agreement with the work of ancient and modern Rabbis (and many Christians as well!). Both schools see the days of creation as 6,000 years followed by a radical change in God's manner of dealing with fallen man and the curse that has been placed on creation (Genesis 3).

Recall that the Scripture teaches that things on earth are a shadow of things in Heaven (Hebrews 8:5), and Peter reminds us that one day with the Lord is as 1,000 years (II Peter 3:8).

Also, Psalm 90:4 says:

> *"For a thousand years in your sight*
> *Are like a day that has just gone by."*

It is not difficult from this perspective to see allegorical prophecy in the account of creation given in Genesis. There are six days of creation (Genesis 1) followed by a Holy day of rest. Thus, the prophetic extension of six days to 6,000 years of fallen creation, followed by a <u>day</u> of rest - 1,000 years of peace, the millennium [Rest in the Messianic Kingdom.]

There are several examples of this seven (7) day picture seen in the life of Jesus. In the Gospel of John we find the sign given at the wedding feast at Cana (John 2). I reinforce "sign" vice "miracle" because the work of the Messiah was more than a parlor trick or even a 'simple' miracle (extension of the laws of fallen creation). The work of Messiah was to do the will of the Father - and thereby to show who He (Jesus) was and where He came from (Heaven/God) and exactly what "time" it was prophetically. In the sign of the wedding feast, note that the miracle occurs on the seventh day. Follow the days of Chapter 1 carefully. On the fourth day, Jesus takes a trip to Galilee. If this sign is a program/paradigm of the creation days sequence, then day 4 is 4,000 years into creation and the trip to Galilee represents the first coming of Jesus and the wedding at Cana on day seven is the second coming of Jesus and the wedding feast is the marriage of the Bride of Christ. The entire "sign" is prophecy showing the design of the Plan of God. (I am indebted to Joseph Good for this chronological/eschatological picture!).

In Matthew 17, we see the transfiguration of Jesus. Note the phrase in Verse 1: *"After 6 days."* These are the six days of fallen man (and creation) which take 6,000 years. Then the 1,000 years of Jesus in transfigured glory. So here again is a picture of creation ending in the Kingdom of the Messiah.

If these examples are indeed pointers and prophecy of a 6,000-year period followed by 1,000 years of rest, then many major events in Scripture (the Rapture and the tribulation, for example) must occur quite soon.

5.0 GOD'S CLOCK

If you have a plan you usually have a schedule and if you have a schedule you usually have a clock. That way you'll know when and, therefore, where you are. God's Plan has a clock too.

As we pointed out earlier, the feasts instituted by God (on a calendar designed by God) are rehearsals of the actual events - pre-ordained for a specific hour, day , month, year - <u>Mo`ed</u> - appointed. [Appointed from eternity.] (See Strong's Exhaustive Concordance of the Bible; Hebrew and Chaldee Dictionary reference entry 4150.)

God's first use of the word "Mo`ed" in Scripture is in Genesis 18:14b. In speaking of the promise to Abraham:

> *I will return to you at the appointed time*
> *next year and Sarah will have a son*

God knew the very day and hour of Isaac's birth. And the Word says in Exodus 12:41: (Also of God's promise to Abraham):

> "At the end of the 430 years, <u>to the very day,</u>
> all the Lord's divisions left Egypt."

If God did it once "to the very day" He can, and will, surely do it again - <u>to the very day</u>. Yes, all of the Lord's divisions are going to leave Egypt (the world of sin) for the last time - in the twinkling of an eye. PRAISE GOD!!!

In Revelation 9:15, John says of the four angels who were bound at the great River Euphrates, that they:

> "...had been kept ready for this very hour and day and month and
> year."

Sure seems kind of specific and precise to me.

Sir Robert Anderson, a British Theologian of the late nineteenth century, wrote a book on the prophecies of Jesus' return called "The Coming Prince". The work stresses the precision of God's word. It was this belief in the precision of the Lord's Word that caused Sir Robert Anderson such quandary in the interpretations of Daniel's 70 weeks. Anderson worked on the prophecy for some time before he discovered God's clock. Since this prophecy is about Jesus and His first coming, let's take a closer look.

We see in Daniel's prophecy (Daniel 9:25ff) that God says to the prophet (and therefore also to us):

"Know and Understand This"

If God gives us a command to 'know and understand' something, then it surely seems reasonable to go ahead and try to learn that teaching. We should learn all of the Word (even Chronicles) with equal vigor; but being just flesh, we learn the parts we like the best. But it does seem reasonable that if God says "HEY LOOK AT THIS!!" that the least a prudent man would do is to pursue the lesson with more than cursory interest. So let's take a look; even if you hate math, try and get this!!!

God says that it will be "Seven sevens and sixty-two sevens until the Anointed One will be cut off." The term "sevens" as used here, means "units of seven" or periods of seven years [some writers call these units of seven years "weeks" of years]. So seven sevens and sixty-two sevens makes sixty-nine sevens (7+62 = 69) or 69 X 7 = 483 years until the unspeakable - the long-awaited and eagerly expected Messiah (the Anointed One) would arrive on Israel's stage and be cut off, i.e. KILLED!

[Note: The Hebrew word used for cut - kârath - means to cut down or cut off (by implication: to destroy or consume). Kârath is used specifically with regard to covenant, eg. The cutting into pieces of the animals one would walk between as a pledge of fidelity to the bargain or treaty (as Abraham did in Genesis 15:9-17). See Strong's Hebrew and Chaldee Dictionary entry 3772. Therefore regarding Messiah, the prophecy language cut off (kârath) means slaughtered (sacrificed) for the purpose of covenant. Thank you, Jesus!]

The promised redeemer of Genesis 3:15, who would crush Satan's head, would be killed. The grand hero of Israel would be rejected! How can this be?

Isaiah said He would be "despised and rejected by men." (Isaiah 53:3). And so He was. But the 483 years was a problem. Just when was all of this to happen?

Daniel 9:25 says we should start counting (start the clock) "from the issuing of the decree to rebuild Jerusalem" not just with streets and houses, but with "defenses". [The King James Version says "walls" and the NIV says "trench" (or literally "teeth") but the concept is the same - a city with walls, gates and able to defend itself.]

The decree that Daniel's prophecy is referring to is the decree given by King Artaxerxes to Nehemiah. Artaxerxes was the son of Xerxes, the Grand Persian monarch, who had dreams of conquering Greece and the Western World around 480 BC. Artaxerxes was a wise ruler and was sympathetic to the needs of the people in the lands conquered by his father. He was especially sensitive to the needs of the Jews (he would have known Esther – his father's queen - and possibly Mordecai – Esther's uncle – see the book of Esther). Artaxerxes gave one of his palace servants, a talented man named Nehemiah, a decree to go and rebuild the city of Jerusalem - to rebuild it's walls and gates too! Artaxerxes even helped pay for the project. (See Nehemiah 2:1-9)

Nehemiah and the Jews had many enemies in the lands around Jerusalem. The Holy Spirit of God spoke of this in the prophecy.

Note: Consider the prophecy's reference to "troublous times" and recall how Nehemiah had to build the wall with armed sentinels on duty and every worker armed and ready to fight! Troublous times indeed. Interested readers are encouraged to read about the great wall building adventure in the Scripture book of Nehemiah. The political scene that is portrayed is filled with intrigue and deceit. Things haven't changed much in 2,500 years.

History gives the 20th year of King Artaxerxes' reign as 445 BC. If we take this year (445 BC) as our starting point, then if we go forward through history and through time 483 years, the prophecy says we will find "Messiah comes."

Well, 445 BC plus 483 years takes us to 39 AD - well past the time of Jesus or His crucifixion. Was something "wrong" with the Scriptures? Other expositors attempted to link the prophecy to Jesus' birth or other temporal events using extra biblical sources for their decree (starting point) but Anderson was sure that if God said "HEY LOOK AT THIS!" (i.e., "know and understand"), then all the data he needed to solve the problem would be found in the Holy

Scripture - the Holy Spirit would have provided the answer somewhere.

And He had!

Anderson was sure that the prophecy of Daniel was accurate because it was "The Word of <u>God</u>" who cannot lie. Then why would the prophecy indicate a time of 39 AD for the crucifixion?

Anderson found the key to the riddle in the story of Noah and the flood. In Genesis 7, Verse 11-12, it says:

> *"...on the seventeenth day of the second month - on that day all*
> *the springs of the great deep burst forth, and*
> *the floodgates of the heavens were open. And rain fell on the*
> *earth forty days and forty nights." .*

Later in Verses 3 and 4 of Chapter 8, the Word of the Lord says:

> *"...at the end of the hundred and fifty days the water had gone*
> *down, and on the seventeenth day of the seventh month, the*
> *ark came to rest on the mountains of Ararat." .*

Anderson realized that the period of time described in Genesis was exactly five months [from the 17th day of the 2nd month to the 17th day of the 7th month] and the Scripture says this was 150 days. Since a 'month' was one cycle of the moon, then 5 months of exactly 150 days means 30 days per lunar month! But the lunar calendar in Anderson's day (circa 1880) did not have 30 days per month, it had 29.5. In fact, as far back in recorded history as one might care to check, the lunar synodic period (from New Moon to New Moon), was found to be 29.5 days. [Current measurements place the "mean" or average lunar month at 29.530588 days].

Five months of 29.5 days would be 147.5 days or rounded up at 148 days, but not 150 days. And that was the answer! Anderson realized that when God spoke in "prophetic time," He used a clock - a lunar clock - of **30** days per month and 360 days per year (not the 365-1/4 days per year we use in our calendar).

If one looks elsewhere in Scripture, you can find confirmation of Anderson's observation.

Daniel 7:25 refers to a period of time when Satan will attack the believers as time, times and half a time (i.e., 3-1/2 years).

John, in the Book of The Revelation, confirms this prophecy in 12:14. But previously in 12:6, John explains that this same period prophesied by Daniel (time, times and half a time) was a period of 1260 days. If we have a prophetic year of 360 days in view, then 1260 days divided by 360 equals 3-1/2 years. And if we are talking about 30 days per month, then this period is 1260/30 = 42 months exactly. In Revelation 11:2-3, John also equates 42 months with a period of 1260 days. Therefore, "a month" to God equals 30 days.

[Why a month to God is 30 days and a year is 360 days, is discussed later in Chapter 6.]

With the insight that a prophetic month was 30 days and a prophetic year of 12 months was 360 days, Anderson was now able to calculate Daniel's prophecy of 69 weeks to Messiah more accurately. "69 weeks" is (as shown earlier) 69 X 7 years or 483 years. But this is 483 **prophetic** or **"Holy years"** as Anderson called them - years of 360 days each. Therefore, the time to Messiah computes to 483 X 360 = 173,880 days!

Using the same starting point as before (1st Nisan 445 BC - the issuing of the decree to rebuild Jerusalem given by Artaxerxes to Nehemiah - see Nehemiah Chapter 2), Anderson converted the lunar calendar to the Julian (solar) calendar and started to count the days and years at 365 for a normal year and 366 days (a February 29th) for a leap year - except for years ending in 00 - for this year there is no Leap Day (unless it is divisible by 400. If the year ending in 00 is divisible by 400 then the year is a leap year). Anderson's complicated approach provided the exact day the prophecy said, "Messiah will come."

This detailed technique of Anderson's also answered another question. The prophecy says Messiah will come - well one might ask "Will come where?" or "Will come how?"

The 173,880th day fell on the 10th of Nisan in the year 32 AD. From Exodus 12 we know that the 10th of Nisan is the day that the Passover Lamb is taken into the house. This day, the 10th of Nisan is Jesus' triumphal entry (on the back of a donkey [Zechariah 9:9]) into the city and His entrance into the house - the house of the Lord - my Father's house - the Temple in Jerusalem. (See

Matthew 21)

We can approximate Anderson's work by simply taking the 483 prophetic Holy years until "Messiah will come" and multiply them by (what I will call) Anderson's conversion factor [A]=360/365.25. This rough technique will not give us "to the day" accuracy like the day-to-day counting method, but it will give the reader a sense of what is happening.

If we take the prophetic 483 Holy years and multiply by (360 ÷ 365.25) we get 476.057, or just a hair over 476 years.

Beginning as we did originally with the twentieth year of King Artaxerxes, or 445 BC, and going forward in time 476 years, we get the year 32 AD (Remember to add 1 more year to the Algebra of 476 - 445 = 31 because there is no year "zero". The Julian calendar goes from 1 BC to 1AD... with no year "zero", so the math is 476 - 445 = 31 (+1) = 32 AD.)

Since we started at the beginning of the month of Nisan in 445 BC, we now arrive at the beginning of Nisan in the year 32 AD. The decimal remainder of .057 takes us a number of days into the month of Nisan (the 10th would be perfect!) but the lunar calendar and the solar Julian calendar can vary from year to year by up to 20 or so days. In this example .057 x 365 = 21 days, which is 11 days past our correct target of the 10th. But the answer is within our error limit of ± 20 days. Extra lunar months are added to the Jewish calendar every few years to correct this variance with the solar calendar. This complicated calendar resolution question is too complex for the scope of this work. But what we have shown is that the prophecy of Daniel, which speaks of 69 weeks of years, means 483 <u>prophetic Holy years</u>. To convert this original metric of God's clock to our calendar we can multiply by 360/ 365.25 to get a very close approximation (less than .005% error); or we can compute the precise answer by Anderson's method of counting the days (and years and leap days and leap years).

The main point of all of this is quite simple: God's prophetic word, which He Himself holds up as the yard stick of His time transcendent omniscience, is precise.

We just need to use the same clock; God's clock - the Moon!

6.0 MYSTERIES OF THE MOON

We will examine a number of other prophecies that are based on God's clock. The centerpiece of that time marking system is the lunar cycle. We know today that the mean, or average, lunar month is 29.53 days. The actual synodic lunar cycle from new moon to new moon will vary somewhat, the 29.53 days is just the average. Under certain orbital conditions the measured value would vary by up to 13 hours. So any given cycle could have up to 30 days or as few as 29 days - but the average over many cycles will be 29½ days. Twelve lunar months then would not work out to 360 days but rather 354 days, give or take. Why would God's Word say 360 days to a lunar year when we can see and measure 354 days to a lunar year and 365¼ days to a solar year?

Well God didn't say there were 30 days in a lunar month <u>today</u> - He said there were 30 days in a lunar month at the time of Noah. Noah's great adventure with the flood occurred about 1656 years after creation. This figure can be reached by adding the years of "Fatherhood" given in Genesis 5:3-28 to the age of Noah given in Genesis 7:6 as shown in Table 6-1. (Also see Appendix I Error Analysis for a discussion on the accuracy of this approach.)

Adam to Seth	130
Seth to Enosh	105
Enosh to Kenan	90
Kenan to Mahalalel	70
Mahalalel to Jared	65
Jared to Enoch	162
Enoch to Methuselah	65
Methuselah to Lamech	187
Lamech to Noah	<u>182</u>
Years to Noah	1056
Noah's age at flood	<u>600</u>
Year of the Flood	1656 after creation.

Table 6-1

THE FLOOD YEAR

Using James Ussher's year of creation as 4004 BC, we find the year of the flood as 2,348 BC.

> [NOTE: There are a variety of folks who believe God created our world but who have a hard time with the "young earth" theory. The secular world bangs on our faith constantly, telling us how the earth is 5 billion years old and how evolution was "the force" that developed life and how man has been quasi-civilized for 8,000 years - and on and on it goes.]

Some very sincere believers are moved by certain arguments (in dating and archeological history) and accept concepts of "age" that are a few thousand to many millions of years out of step with the Scripture story. For these folks, I have two cautions:

1. Don't forget "The Curse!" (Genesis 3) Whatever we see today that involves "decay" or "corruption" comes from the curse. That means that the "processes" of corruption that cause decay were not present before the curse - in Paul's words, "The whole creation groans." (See Romans 8:18-22.)

2. Peter cautions us, using the most serious tones, to consider the scoffers who doubt Christ's coming when he says:
   "But they deliberately forget that long ago by God's word the heavens existed and the earth was formed out of water and by water. By these waters also the world of that time was deluged and destroyed." 2 Peter 3:5,6

Whatever "model" you chose for your creation's picture, please include the effects of the curse and the flood. If that model does not fit the 7,000 year plan presented here, so be it - but don't throw the baby out with the bath water - the curse is real and the flood is real history - at least Jesus thought so [maybe He was wrong? Really!??] So in one worldview, the young earth creation view, the flood was about 2348 BC.

People who think of the age of the earth in these terms are called "literal" or "young earth" Creationists. Within the creationists' school (those who believe God "created" the heaven's and the earth according to the "six days" of creation), there are many theories and doctrines about exactly how long the "six days" were and exactly how long ago this happened. There are even believers in God who hold to the theories of evolution and a very agéd earth - about 5 billion years old.

The purpose of this text is not to examine the strengths and weaknesses of each position. Neither is it our job to determine what is acceptable as "data" or whether or not the physical laws regarding time, the speed of light, work and energy have remained constant over the life of the universe. These issues we will leave to another apologist.

The author is a "short" or "young earth" Creationist and does believe that the physical laws and processes observable today <u>have changed</u> over the life of the universe and that any attempt to hold these laws as "invariant" for time measurement purposes will result in dramatic errors in calculating the age of pre-historic events. This is because the universe (all physical elements) and man (all spiritual elements) were catastrophically affected by:

1. Sin's entrance into creation, and
2. God's curse on fallen man

Failure to consider these extremely important events as <u>real</u> to the history of the universe and real to the nature of man will force disastrous errors in our physical theories. Similarly, "curse blind" thinking will produce abhorrent errors in social/behavioral theories as well as in our philosophical world-view, as to the <u>purpose</u> of our existence. (Which is of course to bring glory (and honor) to God - which is why anything exists, be it a star, a flower, a mouse or a man).

These arguments, however, are for another book, but we must look at a couple of disturbing facts when we consider the topic of God's clock and the 7,000 year Plan of Salvation.

> [NOTE: The author is very aware that the interpretation of Scripture is not reserved to schools of theology or individuals - no matter how logical or well-meaning (2 Peter 1:20). *"...no prophecy of Scripture came about by the prophet's own interpretation."* The only correct interpretation belongs to the Lord and is given to man through His Holy Spirit. We may not (and must not) develop theories or models which place God "in a box." The workings of the Divine and absolute mind are way beyond our finite capabilities (Ref: Isaiah 55:8*). "...My thoughts are not your thoughts..."*

But God <u>does</u> say *"Come now let us reason together."* (Isaiah 1:18). It is my humble prayer that the **WORD** (as interpreted in this text) is rightly divided so that none might be offended, but rather that we are all blessed and God is glorified by and through the light of wisdom, knowledge and understanding - His light and His purpose...Amen.]

If, in fact, the Rabbis and theologians are correct in the interpretation of 6,000 years for fallen man and 1,000 years of restoration, then there should be some evidence that a "young earth" theory is reasonable. We are going to look at two mysteries concerning the moon and this question of "age."

First, there is the dust on the lunar surface - or more precisely, the <u>lack</u> of adequate dust accumulation (accretion) for an object that is considered to be "old." The arguments over how deep the dust was on the lunar surface were tossed about hot and heavy in the years just prior to the first satellite and manned landings. [Interested readers should consult both the secular periodicals and the engineering journals of the early 60's to find a fuller treatment of the subject].

An object without an atmosphere (like our moon) does not undergo terrestrial weathering. It has no "weather" in the conventional use of the word. Solar radiation beats unmercifully on the surface and continual bombardment by meteorites both large and small, act to pulverize the surface to dust. One would think that 5 billion years of such treatment would create a very significant amount of dust on the surface. Before the first landings, some scientists had dust depth estimates as high as 50 meters (over 150 feet of dust!).

But when Neil Armstrong made the first human footprints on Mare Tranquillitatis they were only about 1 centimeter to 1 inch deep. That's a long way from 50 meters - and a long way from any conclusive average. 1 cm is so small an accretion (build-up) as to be no accretion at all!!

[Note: The dust depth in the lunar highlands was, as expected, deeper than on the maria - 2 to 3 inches - but this is still a very small amount for so very long a time.]

You know how fast dust accumulates in your attic or garage - how much would be there after 5 billion years?!

Another more troubling bit of knowledge that came out of the Apollo lunar missions was the distance to the moon. Laser reflectors left on the moon gave earth-bound scientists a precise way to measure the separation between the Earth and moon. But guess what?! It wasn't a stable fixed distance! The distance kept growing with each measurement - not a lot, but a detectable increase of 4" (inches) every year. Since Neil Armstrong landed in July of 1969, to this writing, (December of '96), the moon has receded from the Earth by over 9 feet. Now that's not very far when you consider that the moon is almost a quarter of a million miles away - but the forces involved to separate the Earth and the moon must be strong enough to overcome the attractive force of gravity that holds the Earth and moon together. These forces must be very large. The moon's mass is about 7×10^{22} kg. The Earth's gravity at the lunar distance is greatly reduced, but it is still about .00025 of that here on the Earth's surface, so the moon's "weight" is about 2×10^{16} tons. (20,000,000,000,000,000 tons). It takes a lot of force to move that much weight.

Geophysicists working on planetary studies believe that this increasing earth/lunar separation is caused by the tidal bulge that accumulates because the oceans (here on earth) are blocked from flowing together by the continents. If there were no continents in the way, we would have a more uniform sea level. But as it is now, the Atlantic Ocean is about 3/4 foot lower than the Pacific Ocean's mean sea level. This difference is made more dramatic by tidal change which can put the Pacific Coast sea level of the Americas over 10 feet above the Atlantic Coast mean sea level for the same continents. The effects of this variable fluid environment cause an off-center pull on the moon by the sloshing oceans. Figure 6-1 greatly simplifies this problem.

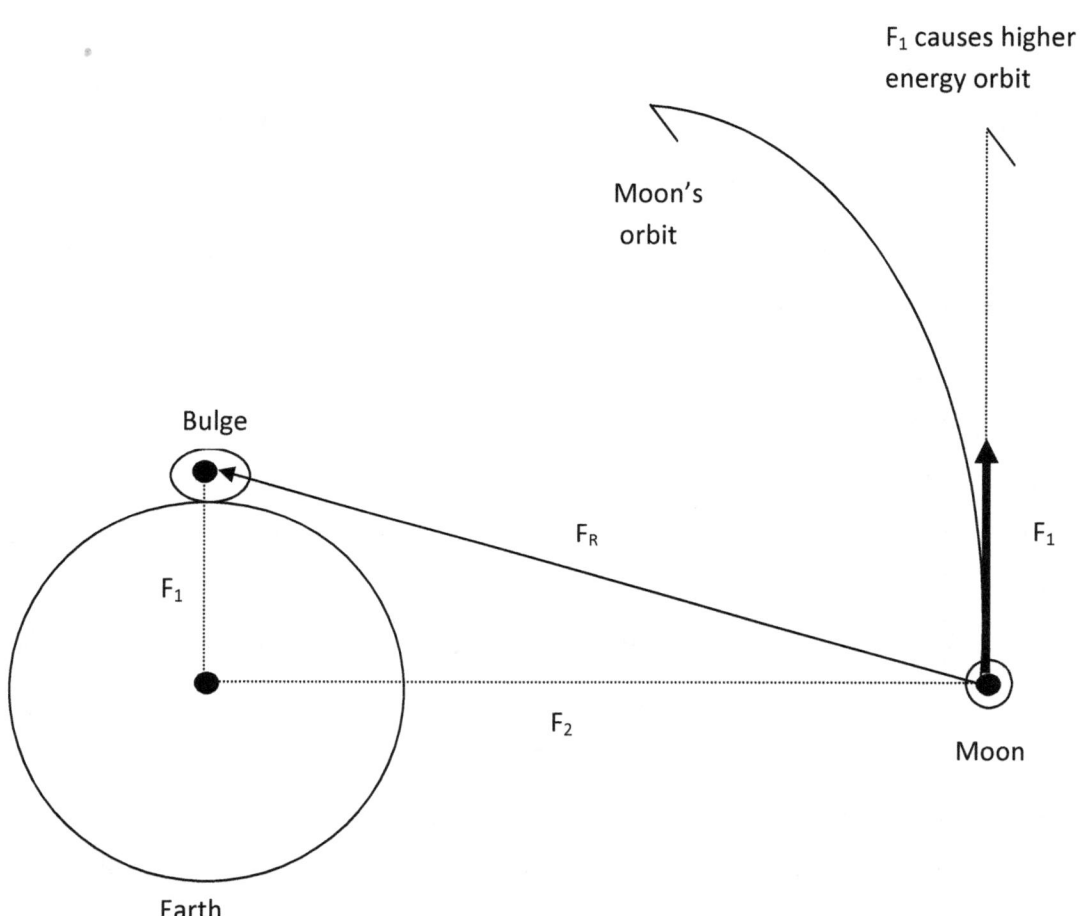

FIGURE 6-1

EARTH - MOON ORBIT DIAGRAM

In Figure 6-1, the gravitational force between the bulge and the moon, lies along line "FR" (force resultant). But we know from first year physics that we can treat this resultant force as if it were made up of two small forces acting at 90° that provide the same effect (i.e., have the same results) (=resultant force). This breakdown gives us "F_1" and "F_2".

Now F_2 lies along the same path as the major Earth-Moon gravity force, but force F_1 (at 90° to force F_2) is seen acting as if it is pulling the moon forward - thus the F_1 component is <u>adding</u> energy to the moon's orbit which increases the distance from the Earth to the moon - by 4 inches per year.

This quite modest increase in the Earth-moon separation distance is so small that it has almost no significance. One is tempted to say "so what!" The significance is more profound, however, if one asks how long has this been going on?

Let's look at the cumulative effect of this 4" per year by letting time run backwards. By doing this, we learn that at the end of last year, the moon was 4" closer to Earth than it was when the year started. A hundred years ago the moon was 400" (or 33-1/3 feet) closer to the Earth than today. Continuing back in time even further, a thousand years ago, the moon was 333 feet closer and a million years ago, it was 333,333 feet closer (or a little over 63 miles closer to the earth).

Now comes the fun stuff. A billion years is 1000 million years. So one billion years ago (if anyone can imagine such a length of time), the moon was 63,000 miles closer than today. If this process continued for 3.8 billion years, the moon would collide with the earth.

> [NOTE: There is a "practical" limit to how close a moon can move to it's parent planet called Roche's Limit. At that distance (which for the Earth and moon is about 10,000 miles), the force of gravity between the bodies literally tears the moon to pieces. This is what happened to some of the moons of Saturn. They became the beautiful rings of moon fragments].

So back to our "age of the moon" question. Both the shallow dust depth on the moon and the 4" per year separation rate tell us that the process ongoing today <u>cannot</u> be characteristic of a 5 billion year old process. Both processes have to be '<u>recent</u>'. How long have these processes been on going? We don't know. In the case of the lunar dust accretion of 1cm to 1 inch, it seems from a casual observation, not very long - only 6,000 years? Perhaps!

And for the increasing Earth-moon separation of 4" per year - maybe that's not happening at all!! Maybe the speed of light is <u>decreasing</u> by 8 centimeters per second per year. Such a slowing in the speed of light would cause the 'apparent' 4 inches of orbital increase for the moon. But even more significantly, it would also account for the "apparent" expansion of the universe known as the Big-Bang theory. If the "red shift" observable in the light from distant galaxies is caused by a decrease in the speed of Light (- C) then both the size and the age of the universe found by evolutionist theory is very inaccurate. The case of Genesis 3 causes all processes to end in disorder. This disorder is called entropy – it is the 2nd law of thermodynamics. Walls collapse, roads crumble, concrete cracks – why should the speed of light (C) be exempt from the laws of entropy? Is the "Big Bang" hypothesis the only workable model?

Perhaps 'space' itself offers a minute resistance to the transmission of light only detectable over intergalactic distances. If the velocity remains constant at C, then the energy loss is detected as frequency loss…hence a red shift. Is there no universal expansion, only universal absorption which is detected as the 3 degree Kelvin background emission? Can this be? Could our universe really be only 6,000 years old? Perhaps! [Good stuff for another book, huh?!!!]

7.0 ANDERSON'S CONVERSION FACTOR AND CAPTIVITY

Anderson's conversion factor [A], which converts prophetic Holy years to our regular Julian years, was not just a convenient mathematical way to adjust numbers and thereby make Scripture prophecy work. If it was just a gimmick, then Anderson would be guilty of 'gross deception'. No - the conversion factor was a product of careful analysis of what was in the Scripture. But was this a unique situation? Would this conversion technique work on other prophecy? The answer is YES, and we will examine other intervals in both fulfilled and as yet unfulfilled convergent prophecy to illustrate the reliability in using [A].

Test Case: Jeremiah's 70 Year Prophecy:

In Jeremiah 25, the Lord says that the captivity of Israel will last 70 years. The fulfillment of this prophecy will be examined again in later sections of this text. But right now, let's look just at the dates involved and use Anderson's conversion factor to see if history supports God's prophecy.

The secular and pagan educators of this world will tell you that Scripture is just man-made stories used for teaching ethics or morality (morality, from a nomadic, male, Jewish perspective!). They will never say that the Scripture is the transcendent, inerrant Word of God. The 70-year prophecy of Jeremiah is often used to show that Scripture is not accurate (sometimes not even approximate) and only represents a poetic concept, not **'truth'**.

Nebuchadnezzar, the King of Babylon, attacked and destroyed the City of Jerusalem in 586 BC. The survivors of this attack were taken into captivity and transported back to Babylon to become workers in the Chaldean society. These Jews remained captives of the Babylonians until the empire collapsed and fell to the Medo-Persians in 539 BC. The Jews were released the following year in 538 BC.

Skeptics are quick to point out that from 586 BC to 538 BC is only 48 years, not 70 years. Therefore, biblical prophecy must be taken with a grain of salt - it's not truth, it's poetry; it's not God's Word, it's cultural literature, nice stories, etc.

There are also, among the learnéd, a more understanding group that realize the prophecy covers more events than just the destruction of Jerusalem. The armies of Nebuchadnezzar made three large forays against the Jews trying to bring them into submission <u>without</u> destroying the Nation.

Israel refused to pay tribute to Nebuchadnezzar and attempted to break away from Babylon in 606 BC. Israel saw the power of Egypt, their southern neighbor, as the saving grace. Nebuchadnezzar marched south in the spring of 605 BC and destroyed the Egyptian pretender at the Battle of Charchemish. A detachment of his army advanced on Jerusalem and carried off into captivity the ruling class elite who were encouraging the tax rebellion. The prophet Daniel was among the group taken in 605 BC. Nebuchadnezzar also attacked Jerusalem (for attempted rebellion to his rule) in 598 BC. This time he carried into captivity all of the upper class, royalty, priesthood and learnéd members of the society. Only craftsmen, farmers and peasants were left. This last group was all but annihilated in the 587-586 BC siege and sacking of the city.

The 70-year prophecy, therefore, covered the period of captivity beginning in 605 BC and ending, say the historians, in 538 BC. From 605 to 538 is 67 years. This is closer to the prophetic 70 but still not exactly 70, so Bible prophecy is still only poetic, not absolute.

Later in this text we will develop the reasons why 538 BC (the date of the Jews' release from captivity in Babylon) is not the end point of the prophecy. The nation of Israel went into captivity for failing to honor God. Jerusalem and the Temple were destroyed because of idol worship. It is not until events in the spring of 536, when the same Jews are back in the ruins of Jerusalem, that the prophecy finds its fulfillment. This is explained and supported in Chapter 9. But for now, let's work with Spring 536 as an accepted termination point. Therefore:

Captivity begins	Spring 605 BC (month = Ziv or May)
Captivity ends	Spring 536 BC (month = Ziv or May)
Total length	69 years

This period of 69 years is almost historically exact. It is accurate to the month. (Closer accuracy is not possible because we don't know how many days before or after the Battle of Charchemish that Daniel was taken captive).

So the historic record shows 69 years almost to the day and God said 70 years. Is the Bible still wrong? NO! God's 70 years are **prophecy.** Therefore, we have to use Anderson's conversion factor to convert 70 prophetic Holy years of 360 days/year to Julian calendar years of 365-1/4 years. If Anderson's technique proved a precise fulfillment for Daniel's 70 weeks, will it work on Jeremiah's 70 years? (Oh, yes it will!)

$$\frac{70 \times 360}{365.25} = 68.994 \text{ Julian years}$$

68.994 years is less than 48 hours from 69 historic years and since our historic record is only accurate to the month, the conversion is within the error limit and may be said to work exactly.

Anderson's technique will be used many times in this text and will consistently provide accurate conversions of prophecy to Julian years.

But why is this [A] conversion factor necessary in the first place? That's because the length of the day and the length of the month have changed since the days of Noah and the flood. These changes in the length of the day and month will be examined in some detail in Chapter 8.

8.0 SIGNS IN THE HEAVENS

8A THE DAY OF THE COMET

[NOTE: If you don't like math, skip this chapter - it's only for hypothetical example!]

The earth completes one orbit - one trip around the sun - every 31,558,149.5 seconds. We call this period a "year." But while the earth is traveling the nearly 600 billion-mile circuit, it is also spinning on its axis. Each complete spin, we call one "day."

So when we speak of the number of days to a year, we are really talking about the number of spins that are completed while one very long trip around the Sun is completed. Today the Earth completes 365.25 spins for one trip around the Sun - 365 ¼ spins = 365 ¼ days. But at the time of Noah, God tells us that the number of days per year was 360. It is not the length of the year that has changed (i.e. gotten longer by 5 ¼ days), but rather that the Earth today is spinning faster - so much faster that it completes 5 ¼ more spins per trip around the Sun than it used to at the time of Noah. This is an increase of about 1.5% in the number of total spins (i.e., number of "days") per year.

What could cause such an increase? Could it have anything to do with the flood? Almost certainly! The conditions on the Earth at the time of Noah were remarkably different from today. Before the flood, it had never rained!!

God watered the Earth with a heavy mist (see Genesis 2:6). The atmosphere was very humid and the sky was overcast. Notice how God refers to the Sun and Moon as the Greater Light and the Lesser Light in Genesis 1:16. Seen through a heavy fog, the Sun and Moon would not be directly visible – hence Greater Light and Lesser Light. This picture is reinforced by Genesis 1:6 which says, "God separated the water above the sky from the water below". Many creationists' theories have been constructed to model this predeluvian environment. The ice canopy model is a classic example. Exploration of all the creationist's models is beyond the scope of this text but we will offer a possible explanation for the increase in the Earth's rotation rate and the tilting of the Earth's axis. We will build this model on recently observed phenomena here in

53

our own solar system.

In 1986, Haley's Comet passed by the Earth in it's 76-year voyage around the Sun. These encounters can be close shaves. During the 1910 rendezvous, the Earth passed through the Comet's tail. There was no danger from this "collision" however, since a comet's tail is very nebulous. A comet is just a big snowball - an accumulation of ice and perhaps some rock that is left over from the days of creation. Some astronomers believe comets have already collided with the earth - most recently in 1908 in the Siberian wilderness of Russia. This 'small' collision destroyed the Siberian forests for several hundred kilometers. In July of 1994, the comet Shoemaker-Levy collided with the planet Jupiter. Jupiter's gravity, combined with other influences, had broken the comet into a series of large fragments - a comet train. These fragments plunged into the Jovian atmosphere over several days.

Could it have been an encounter with a very large comet train that caused the Noahic flood? Perhaps. Let's look at this a little more closely and see if such a model can account for:

1. Severe disruption of the tectonic plates
2. Rain for 40 days.
3. Rate of spin + 1.5%
4. Axis tilt

[NOTE: Please keep in mind that this "model" is being tested just for <u>fun</u>. No attempt is being made here to validate this model--only to see if such a piece of fancy is even within the realm of possibility, i.e. could a collision impact provide enough extra energy to cause the earth to spin faster?]

Step 1: How much water do we need for the flood?

In Genesis 7:11, the Scripture tells us that the *...fountains of the great deep burst forth.* So let's attribute <u>most</u> of the water from this oceanic source. This is important - most of the flood was caused by <u>ground water</u>. Let's say that the Earth (in Noah's day) was basically flat. Let's give Noah's Earth a high point of 1.5 miles, or about 8,000 feet (2.4 km).

If the highest point the flood reached was 2.4 kilometers, then let's allow 2 kilometers of water to come from the fountains of the deep. Then the remaining 400 meters would have to come from the melting ice and snow of the comet. That's still a lot of water.

> [NOTE: It is also assumed here that the Earth's highest mountains (like the Alps, Rockies, Andes and Himalayas) are the <u>results</u> of the flood. These very high mountains were either not there or they were not as high prior to the flood. The huge weight of all that water on the Earth's crust would surely have broken the crust along the mega-fault lines that today separate the major tectonic plates. For example: think about a waterbed - if you push down at one point on a water bed, the rest of the mattress comes up - the crust of the Earth would have behaved the same way. And collisions with massive objects, (like a comet train), could easily smashed through the crust and expose the Earth's inner core. The holes produced by these impacts would definitely account for the fountains of the great deep springing forth].

Step 2: So what is the volume of water that would cover the globe 400 meters deep? The Earth's radius is about 6378 km and the surface area is $4\pi R^2$ = 511 X 10^6 Sq Km (area) X 400 meters deep = 2 X 10^8 cubic kilometers (Km^3) of water! That is a big "ball" of water (comet ice). If it was just one piece, it would be 450 miles across!

If the Earth were the size of a beach ball, our comet would be about the size of a large peanut. But let's break the comet into 20 or 30 pieces, each about the size of a BB. Separate the pieces by a few hours to a few days and we have a comet train like the comet Shoemaker-Levy that recently collided with Jupiter. (But Jupiter is 1,366 times the size of the Earth and over 300 times as massive. The comet's impact had little affect on the massive planet's rotation. (If the Earth is a beach ball, Jupiter is a small truck!)). But could an ice ball (or a series of ice ball fragments) affect the earth's rotation?

Step 3: How much would our comet weigh?

The mass of one cubic meter of water is about 1,000 Kg. A volume of 2×10^8 Km^3 (from step 2) would be 2×10^{17} cubic meters (m^3) with a mass of 2×10^{20} kilograms (Kg). But how much "energy" has been added to the earth?

The Earth can be thought of as a spinning ball - this means that it has certain physical properties. The magnitude of the physical properties we need to know to answer the energy question involves the Earth's "Rotational Inertia" (I) and "Angular Velocity" (W). While they have fancy names, these properties (I) and (W) can be derived from better known characteristics such as Mass (M), Radius (R) and the spin rate - the length of day! Let's look at the spin rate change.

Step 4: How much did the spin-rate of the Earth change?

The length of the day today gives us 365.25 days per year. A slower spinning Earth at the time Noah, gave us 360 days per year. This means the spin rate increased by about 1.5%

$$\frac{365.25}{360} = 1.1046$$

Today the Earth spins at a rate of 360 degrees (one full spin) in 24 hours. That is 15 deg/hr or .25 deg/min or 41.67 10^{-4} deg/sec. This spin rate is called "Angular velocity" = (W) [the number of "angles" per second]. Physicists don't use degrees to measure angles, they use "radians" (R) where 1 radian is about 57.3 degrees. The spin rate for the Earth (today) therefore is about W = 7.29×10^{-5} r/s (radians per second)

What was the spin rate (W) <u>before</u> the hypothetical collision?

$$\frac{w}{1.0146} = \frac{7.29 \times 10^{-5}}{1.0146} = 7.185 \times 10^{-5} \ r/s$$

To increase the spin rate would require a big push from the comet.

Step 5: How big was the push from the comet?

To get the Earth to spin faster required that some energy was added to the "system". (This is the amount of rotational energy, or kinetic energy (energy in motion) that was added to the system. This is the "push" provided by the earth/comet collision). The kinetic energy of a rotating mass is found by multiplying the rotational inertia (I) by the square of the angular velocity (W) and dividing by 2. Okay - what is the rotational inertia (I) of the Earth? For a solid sphere the value of I is

$$"I"sphere = \frac{2MR^2}{5}$$

the Earth is not exactly a uniformly solid sphere, but we are only trying to see if a comet could have been the cause of the flood - so we will use the value of I for a sphere.

The mass of Earth $M = 6 \times 10^{24}$ Kg
and the radius $R = 6378$ Km
Therefore:

$$I \cong \frac{2(6 \times 10^{24})(4 \times 10^{13})}{5} = 9.6 \times 10^{37} \text{ J (joules)}$$

[NOTE for the "purist": The rotational inertia of the Earth before the comet hits is not the same as the value of (I) after the comet hits. This is because the mass of the comet adds to the mass of Earth a tiny fraction and adds to the radius of the Earth another tiny fraction. But these are very small fractions and when multiplied together, become extremely small so they may be ignored.]

We know from Step 4 that the angular velocity (W) of the Earth today is 7.29×10^{-5} r/s. Let's call this W_F, the final spin rate. And we also know from Step 4 that the original spin rate was 7.185×10^{-5} r/s. Let's call this W_O, the initial spin rate. Now our formula for the kinetic energy of a rotating sphere is

$$E = \frac{1}{2} I W^2$$

The change in energy (the push from the comet) is found by subtracting from the Earth's energy today (final) the value of E at the time of Noah (initial). Since (I) remains essentially unchanged, all of the push (energy change) can be found from the change in W (spin rate).

$$E = \frac{1}{2} I (W_F^2 - W_O^2) = \frac{9.6 \times 10^{37}}{2} [(7.29 \times 10^{-5})^2 - (7.18 \times 10^{-5})^2] = (4.8 \times 10^{37})(1.52 \times 10^{-10})$$

Push = 7.3 x 10^{27} joules

Step 6: How fast was the comet moving in order to give the earth this much push?

[Note: We happily ignore the many avenues of kinetic energy distribution such as heat loss, inelastic compressions, atmospheric disturbances and such. We are not trying to model all the gory details, only see if such a collision could have the required "push".]

All the new energy added to the Earth's system had to come from the comet's kinetic energy, which is one-half the product of the comet's mass (M), times the square of the comet's velocity (V):

$$E = \frac{1}{2}MV^2$$

From Step 4, we know the mass of the snowball comet was 2X 10^{20} Kg, and from Step 5, the energy change is 7.3X 10^{27} j. Therefore,

$$V^2 = \frac{(2)(7.3 \times 10^{27})}{2 \times 10^{20}}$$

$$V^2 = 7.3 \times 10^7 \text{ m}^2 / \text{s}^2$$

$$V = 8.5 \text{ km/s}$$

or about 5 miles per second.

Step 7: Can a comet travel that fast?

Oh yes! Objects move through our solar system at very high speeds (relative to freeway traffic). The Earth travels around the Sun at 18.5 miles per second! Some large objects exceed even this speed. Mercury, for example, orbits the Sun at 30 miles/sec.

The real test here is whether a comet train could cause the changes and events needed to cause the flood. If our hypothetical comet train took 40 days to complete the collision process, we see continued, or protracted, types of phenomena that meet our criteria.

When we look at the Moon's surface we see the severe scaring from collisions with large bodies passing near the Earth. Most of these objects are gone today, having fallen into the Sun or been destroyed in collisions with other moons or planets. But in the years just after creation, these objects were common. An off-axis collision may have tilted the Earth's axis and caused the flood process at the same time.

So our hypothetical comet — though large by the standards of what remains today – could have existed in pre-history and hit the Earth with:

1. Enough energy to add +1.48% to the spin rate.
2. Provided enough water to cover the Earth to 400M depths.
3. Broken the tectonic plates on the Earth's crust.
4. Caused massive flooding via the springs of the deep
5. Major climate changes

You might feel that such a collision with a comet, while possible, is unlikely - think again. We just watched Shoemaker-Levy hit Jupiter with the energy of hundreds of millions of hydrogen bombs and the small un-named comet of 1908 hit good old earth (and flattened several hundred square kilometers of Siberia.) Because this collision was in a remote part of the world, few people realized it occurred. If the impact point had been in London or New York, it would have been the greatest tragedy in the history of the world (besides the Noahic flood!), killing perhaps 20 million people in the blast.

UPDATE: About six months after the initial writing of this work, Earth was re-visited by comet Hale-Bopp (circa April '97). The estimates for this comet's previous perihelion were about 4,350 years ago. This means Hale-Bopp's last visit near Earth was about 2,353 BC.

In Chapter 6 we dated the flood at c.2348 BC. Hale-Bopp (or a close cousin) could well have been a remnant of the "flood comet". How close does Hale-Bopp come to being a perfect match to our flood comet type? Let's take a look:

1. Hale-Bopp's orbit was at 90° to the ecliptic - the plane of the earth's orbit. This type of orbital inclination would cause the comet-train to strike the earth with some North to South Energy - an off-axis hit. This would account for the tilt in the earth's rotational axis.

2. Hale-Bopp's last visit near earth was about 2350 BC, at the time of

Noah! Note: As Hale-Bopp gets closer to the sun, it is easier to see and easier to measure the orbit. However the orbit is perturbed (bent) by Jupiter, Saturn and Earth as the comet approaches (The "new" orbit is "bent" and will take only 2300 years to complete next time) so the measurement of 4350 years for the old orbit was being altered by the other planets gravitational pull even while the measurements were being made. An orbit of 4,355 years (the years since the flood) is very possible for Hale-Bopp.

3. The perihelion for Hale-Bopp (closest approach to the sun) is about 93,000,000 miles. This is right through the Earth's yearly orbit. If, in fact, the 1997 passage of Hale-Bopp went right through the space the Earth will orbit through in September of '97, then pieces of debris left behind by Hale-Bopp (pieces burned off of the nucleus that formed the brilliant tail) will collide with Earth this Fall. This may give us a super annual meteor shower. Meteor showers happen when the earth passes through the space (orbit) of a defunct comet. This occurs about a dozen or so times per year. So comets other than Hale-Bopp have come very close to Earth before. A collision with a comet is not a far-fetched idea that never happened or an event with million-to-one odds. Just look at the moon's pock marked face to see how common collisions once were!

4. Hale-Bopp was 25 miles across at the nucleus (core mass). This is about the size range we were looking for - but not just one piece - a large "comet train" was hypothesized. Could Hale-Bopp ('97) be a chunk of our Noahic comet train that just happened to miss the earth? It's possible! The Bible speaks of "signs in the heavens" before the return of Jesus. And our Lord said it would be 'like in the days of Noah'. Could Hale-Bopp's first return since Noah be more than just coincidence? Is it one of the signs?

8B MOON STRUCK

Today the moon takes 29.53 days to complete one change of phase or complete one lunar cycle - new moon to new moon. But at the time of Noah the new moon took 30 days to accomplish the new moon to new moon cycle. Somewhere during the flood period, while the earth was <u>gaining</u> about 1 ½ % to its spin rate the moon was <u>losing</u> about 1 ½% of it's orbital energy. It would be wonderful if there was some simple way to explain these changes, but that is not the case, even though both changes are defined by Anderson's conversion factor,

$$\text{Note: } \frac{360}{365.25} \cong [A] \cong \frac{29.53}{30}$$

they happened in different arenas. The moon did not simply give the earth some of its energy. But both changes could have been caused by the same mechanism - a collision. The moon has certainly had many such collisions since creation - some of these events were quite large. Just look at the face of the moon for the proof. Could our hypothetical comet train have caused this lunar orbit change as well as the delta in the earth's spin rate? Are these changes of similar magnitude? Could a comet train of the size and velocity necessary to spin-up the earth also be of the right size and velocity to alter the lunar month? Let's see.

Step 1. How has the lunar period changed?
A) The period has gone from 30 days to 29.5 days - will that answer the question?

No! The change from 30 to 29.5 is the delta in the "synodic" period or cycle time. This is the time from full moon to full moon as seen from the earth.

Since both the earth and the moon are moving (around the sun) we need a common fixed reference point. We need to find the change in the "sidereal" period - the length of the moon's orbit as measured against the 'fixed' star background.

We will approximate the Noahic sidereal period by this simple ratio.

$$\frac{\text{synodic then}}{\text{synodic today}} \quad \frac{\text{sidereal then}}{\text{sidereal today}}$$

The moon's sidereal period today is 27.32 days per orbit. So if X = "Sidereal period then" (at the time of Noah) we have the following relation:

$$\frac{30.00}{29.53} = \frac{x}{27.32}$$

thus X = 27.75 days.

OK? No!!! **WRONG!!**

The Noahic period of 27.75 days is 27.75 **OLD days** - 27.75 days at 360 days per year. We must convert this sidereal period to today's clock (which runs 1½% faster). Therefore:

$$P = 27.75/[A] = 28.16 \text{ days}$$

B) Now we know the sidereal period changed from 28.16 days (then) to 27.32 days (today). Can we use these values? Yes!

The formula for the period of an Earth orbiting satellite (like the moon) is found from:

$$P^2 = \frac{4\pi^2 (R_E + d)^3}{GM_E}$$

[Note: This formula assumes that the radius of the satellite is very small when compared to the separation distance. Thus the satellite can be treated as a 'point' object. This is not true for our earth moon problem. The radius of the moon is .004 of the separation distance, but this value is still small enough for our hypothetical estimations.]

Where P = period, G = Newton's gravitational constant, R_E and M_E are the radius of the Earth and the mass of the Earth respectively and d = distance from Earth to the satellite. [It is this value 'd' that has changed.]

We could solve for P in both cases but to save some work, let's put in the values for P and divide "then" by "today". This yields:

$$\frac{(28.16)^2}{(27.32)^2} = \frac{(R_E + d')^3}{(R_E + d)^3}$$

OR

$$1.062 = \left[\frac{R_E + d'}{R_E + d}\right]^3$$

If we take the cube root of both sides we find :

$$1.02 = \frac{R_E + d'}{R_E + d}$$

Now we can solve for the ancient separation distance.

Thus d' = .02R$_E$ + 1.02 d

At the time of Noah, the moon was further away from the Earth by 2% of today's distance (1.02d) plus 2 % of the Earth's radius (.02 R$_E$ = .02 X 6371 Km = 127 Km)

The average Earth moon separation distance today is 238,000 miles or 384,400 Km. Therefore d' would be about 392,000 Km at the time of Noah.

Step 2. How has the total energy of the lunar orbit changed?

To find the energy change we must find the differences in kinetic and potential energies between the initial (zero subscript) and the final (f subscript) values

$$\Delta E = \frac{1}{2}m(V_f - v_o)^2 + GM_m \left(\frac{1}{d_o} - \frac{1}{d_F}\right)$$

By inserting the following values

G	=	6.67 x 10^{-11}	N-m/Kg^2
M	=	5.983 x 10^{24}	Kg
μ	=	7.356 x 10^{22}	Kg
d$_F$	=	384.4 x 10^6	m
d$_o$	=	392.4 x 10^6	m
V$_o$	=	1,012.8	m/s
V$_F$	=	1,023.2	m/s

Note: V$_o$ and V$_F$ are approximated using the orbital circumference divided by the sidereal period.

$$\Delta E = (38.2 \times 10^{22} - 1.56 \times 10^{27})\text{N-m}$$

This expression shows the total change in kinetic energy (which is positive because of a higher orbital velocity) and potential energy (which is negative because the moon lost height (or distance) from the earth). The kinetic term is 5 orders of magnitude below the potential term (10^{22} vs. 10^{27}) number and thus may be ignored. The total energy change is therefore:

$$\Delta E = -1.56 \times 10^{27} \text{ N-m}$$

Step 3. If this energy change came about because of a collision with our hypothetical comet train, how large a piece is required?

The comet fragment would have a kinetic energy of E=1/2 MV² that was equal to E of step 2. Since V was previously found to be 8 Km/sec. The comet's collision mass would be:

$$M = \frac{2E}{V^2} = \frac{3.06 \times 10^{27}}{64 \times 10^6}$$

$$M = 4.78 \times 10^{19} \text{ Kg}$$

If this comet 'fragment' was one snowball it would be about 300 miles across. A collision with an object that large would cause a pretty big bang! But the moon has already been hit by objects that large and survived. Look at the eyes or mouth of the man in the moon!

Our original comet-train had a mass of 2 x 1020 Kg. The lunar requirement would bring the combined mass to 2.5 x 1020Kg (a 20% increase).

So if a comet train struck the Earth at the time of Noah in a manner similar to the Jupiter/Shoemaker-Levy collision of 1994 the events of Genesis 7 **could** well have been the result.

Please remember that this was just a fun exercise. God does not need a comet or an ice canopy or any human conceived hypotheticals for "means". If the Lord said 'Go' the flood waters would 'Go'. But a test for the reasonableness of "means" (mechanical method) is not unwarranted.

9.0 STAGE 2000 - THE LAST DAYS

9A THE REBIRTH OF ISRAEL

The idea that the "end of the age" (and this means life <u>as we know it</u>) is close upon us is a hard concept to swallow. You gaze happily out your window and everything seems okay. Flowers are flowering; birds are birding; spring is springing and all that kind of stuff. **Everything is fine**!

But beyond the backyard fence, there are forces at work that will eventually bring about the events of the Book of The Revelation. The application of Anderson's conversion factor to other test case prophecies (which we will examine later) indicates less than 20 years remain for the close of the ages (both the age of GRACE and the age of LAW - Daniel's 70th week). In the author's opinion it doesn't seem possible for all the so-called "pre-requisites" to take place so quickly in order to set the stage. There just doesn't seem to be enough time. For example, where is this one-world government or the third Temple or the great world-wide famine? Everything seems fine today....I don't see the anti-christ!

I agree <u>in my flesh</u> with most all of the arguments that the 70th week of David cannot start for some protracted time. It will just take too long to set the stage (as we commonly picture it). <u>But major world shaking events happen quickly</u>. There's no way in 1988 I would have believed in the collapse of the Soviet Union in just two years and the collapse of the communist governments in Europe by 1991 - but it happened!

However, there are two events, or rather "trends" in science, that lead the author to believe that the end **must** be soon (sooner than we think?). The "miracle" of "in vitro" fertilization has progressed to the point where animals are artificially nurtured through their complete gestation in laboratory "bottles." Eventually, some disturbed mind will attempt this abomination with a human being - and then "clone" his children, of course.

The advancements in life development life/support sciences brings the specter of Huxley's *Brave New World* right to the threshold of Satanic pride - man is in control! Man is life creating! Man is God!! [GOD FORBID!]

The second area of scientific development is in space travel. Eventually man will press outward to colonize the Moon or Mars or terra-form Venus. But the Scriptures seem to deal with God's plan for man here on earth. These events are apparently restricted to earth. The end therefore, should be close at hand - for we are getting ready to leave the nest. An attempt to colonize Mars will probably happen in the next century.

[Note: Those readers interested in the theological aspects of planetary colonization are encouraged to consult C.S. Lewis' Trilogy: "Out of the Silent Planet" where the earth is quarantined to control the migration of sin.]

I am sure there are other valid observations from diverse areas of human "progress" that scream out in many languages: "Dear God, bring the end soon!" (We see the saints in heaven asking: "How long, sovereign Lord...?") (Revelation 6:10)

When I consider, meditate and pray over the abortion issues, I am amazed that the hand of God has not acted in judgment on America already. But to Moses, He says: "the sin of the Amorites is not yet full" - so it must be here with us also. The perverting effects of sin have caused us humans such misplaced guilt that we scream in reflected horror at the drowning of a dolphin in a tuna net while we flush 20% to 30% of the next human generation down the toilet. [The world can hardly wait for RU486 - WOW! - no record keeping then!! Who will know how many babies (God's babies) will perish?!!!]

Every generation of Christians thinks it is the last [there's pride at work for you!] Even the Disciples caught in the great Roman Diaspora thought the return of Jesus was imminent (It can't get much worse than this!) - so they believed.

The Temple was destroyed, Jerusalem was destroyed - Israel was destroyed. What future was left? [And I'm sure the Europeans that saw the Black Death (that ravaged the 1300's) were equally sure of the imminence and necessity of Christ's return.]

But we have two highly significant pieces of evidence to support the near term contention for the return of our Savior - the <u>Scripture sets two pre-requisites</u> for the end;

1. This gospel must first be preached in all the world (to all nations).
2. The nation of Israel must be re-born.

In case you haven't looked out your prophecy window lately, both of these events have happened in "this generation"! (Praise God!!)

The work of countless devoted missionaries has taken the Word of God into every nation on earth. But this profound sacrifice by the men and women of the 19th and 20th centuries pales in effect when compared to the insidious reach of telecommunications. Virtually every human being, from the last Amazon rain forest dweller to the most remote nomad of the Gobi wilderness, is served by radio today. The gospel can reach almost every radio and TV audience in the world. In late 1996, Billy Graham preached the Word on a multi-link broadcast that reached over 2.5 billion souls (Praise God!).

Sadly there are still many <u>individuals</u> who have never heard the message of good news. But every <u>nation</u> has heard the Word - this Scriptural pre-requisite seems satisfied (Matthew 24:14).

The second pre-requisite, for the return of Jesus, the rebirth of Israel, is even more astounding than the global preaching of the Word. The prophecies concerning the rebirth of Israel abound. Table 9-1 gives a list of a few of these.

Deuteronomy	30:3	Psalm	126:1
Isaiah	1:26	Ezekiel	16:55
	10:21		
	51:11	Hosea	3:5
Jeremiah	12:15		14:7
	16:15		
	24:6	Joel	2:25
	27:22		3:1
	29.10		
	29:14	Amos	9:14
	30:3		
	30:10	Obadiah	:15
	30:18		
	31:4	Micah	5:3
	31:8		
	31:16	Zephaniah	3:20
	32:15	Zechariah	2:12
	32:37		10:6
	42:12		

Table 9A-1
PROPHECIES OF ISRAEL'S RETURN

But the most intriguing prophecy of Israel's re-birth is the prophecy of Ezekiel 4:4-6. That prophecy enumerates Israel's sin punishment as 430 years. Yet the actual time they served in captivity was just 70 years. Where does this 70 years come from? WHY 70 YEARS OF CAPTIVITY? WHAT HAPPENED TO THE REMAINING 360 YEARS?

We read in Jeremiah 25:11 that the penalty for the Israelites unfaithfulness would be captivity for 70 years. This sounds reasonable - a righteous and just God inflicting a punishment that fits the crime! Because it was the Word of God it certainly did happen just as He said it would. But why 70 years? Why not 106 or 37 or whatever? What deep principle of infinite righteousness was at work in a Holy God that established the penalty at 70 years?

A clue is given in 2 Chronicles 36:21 which says "the **land** enjoyed its Sabbath **rests**; all the time of its desolation it **rested**, until the seventy years were completed in fulfillment of the word of the LORD spoken by Jeremiah." Some commentators, understanding that the Scriptures require the **land** to be left fallow once every seven years (Leviticus 25:4) have extrapolated backward and determined that Israel's sin period was therefore 490 years (70x7=490). Others have tied this number (490) to the prophecy of Daniel 9:24, 25 which deals with 70 weeks of years or 490 prophetic years. These two prophecies (Daniel 9:24 and Jeremiah 25:11) are related. One deals with Messiah. The other with **rest**. But in the same chapter of Daniel we have another clue. Daniel 9:2 says

> *"In the first year of his reign, I, Daniel, understood from the Scriptures, according to the word of the LORD given to Jeremiah the prophet, that the desolation of Jerusalem would last seventy years."*

Since 2 Chronicles 36, which tells us about the **land**'s Sabbath **rest**, was probably not written until <u>after</u> the exile, what <u>existing</u> Scriptural insights did Daniel receive? The author prayed for two years about this insight seeking a similar word of knowledge.

There is something "unsatisfying" about the standard answer of 490 years of unfaithfulness that appears in normal commentaries. Israel had been in the **land** since Nisan of 1406 BC, over 800 years before Daniel's captivity (605 BC) and the destruction of the first Temple (586 BC). Applying 490 years to either of these dates for the beginning of the sin period takes us back into the time of Samuel, before Saul or David, and in a manner of speaking, before nationhood.

The author believes strongly that the Lord had a specific identifiable event as the starting point for the "period of unfaithfulness" and also an identifiable event for the terminus of the period. In this way, the 70-year penalty was not just a nice Holy number because it had a 7 in it, but a calculable and determinable number discernible from applied Scripture. But what is the lesson? We are talking about a <u>major</u> event in the history of the Jews - and a <u>major</u> event in covenant theology. God had given the land to the Jews. . . <u>forever.</u> Yet, here He was, evicting His own chosen people and subjecting them to catastrophe and humiliation - captivity by a foreign (pagan) power!! **Impossible!** At least two points must be made of this:

<u>One</u> - there had to be a very good reason to "alter" the existing covenant relationship - and,

<u>Two</u> - there had to be significant events to start and end the process. An apparent "change of plans" of this magnitude had to be well defined.

If you throw your own son or daughter out of the house, it surely should be for a very good reason (a reason the child both <u>understood</u> and <u>acknowledged</u>). So it was with Israel - the key to the issue was <u>"relationship."</u> The words of the covenant said:

> *I will be your God and You*
>
> *will be my people*

The first part of the agreement was abrogated by the beneficiaries themselves, for the Jews chased after strange gods - pagan gods - and thereby forfeited the rights inherent within the household of God - they lost the "inheritance" - they lost the "family farm" - they lost the whole nine yards. But only for 70 years....a punishment and a test. Would the full repentance of heart be there after 70 years in captivity? The reason for the 70 years (vice any other number of years) is based on the Law and the Scripture.

In Ezekiel 4:4-6, the Lord tells us that the sin of Israel was for 390 years and the sin of Judah was for 40 years or a collective total of 430 years (not 490 years as commentators often tell us). But going back 430 years from 605 BC or 586 BC provides no significant starting point. But note, if the 430 year period <u>includes</u> the 70 years of captivity, we find that the **land** not only has its Sabbath **rest,** but that the period of unfaithfulness and the period of penalty were concurrent so that both were fulfilled at the endpoint. As a result, the slate would be clean and fresh start would be available to the people. (See Figure 9-1)

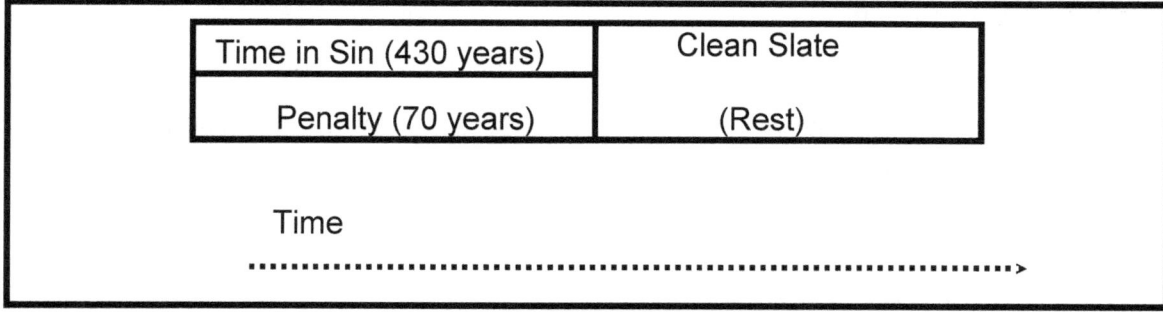

Figure 9A-1

CLEAN SLATE

Leviticus 25:4 tells us the **land** was to have a Sabbath **rest** every seven years. But 430 divided by 7 yields 61.4 years not 70. However, the reader is encouraged to note Leviticus 25:11 which tells us that the **land** should also **rest** for the Jubilee Year, which is Holy and nationally restorative. The Jubilee Year accounts for an additional Sabbath **rest** each 50 years. Dividing 430 years by 50 yields 8.6. When we add all of the Sabbath **rests** together (61.4 + 8.6) we get 70. The reader should also note that year number 350 of the period is both a 7 year Sabbath and a 50-year Jubilee Sabbath (2 in 1) so that only 69 actual **rest** years are required. <u>**This was fulfilled precisely**</u>. We begin when Daniel was taken captive in the spring of 605 BC and continue to the spring of 536 BC. Exactly 69 years! But what is the significant event of 536 BC? The Jews were set free in 538 BC and arrived in Jerusalem in 537 BC. What is so special about the spring of 536 BC?

In Ezra 3:6-10, we read that in the month of Ziv of 536 BC (the second month of the year) the returning exiles began the work of building the Temple - i.e. laying the foundation.

If we go back in time 430 years from this foundation-laying event, we arrive at 1 Kings 6:1. "In the month of Ziv, he began to build the Temple of the Lord." 430 years before 536 BC is the fourth year of Solomon's reign, the year is 966 BC, also the month of Ziv. Thus we see that the period of time for which the **land** required **"rest"** was the period between the first and second Temples. 430 years to the month and possibly to the day. The time between the Temples and the time when the Glory of God was **resting** in and on Israel.

We've seen the Anderson conversion factor produce two precise answers:
1. The exact date for the arrival of the Messiah Jesus' triumphal entry into Jerusalem (10 Nisan 32AD); and,
2. The exact length for the period of Babylonian captivity <u>served</u> - 69 solar years exactly.

Are there other prophecies that Anderson's conversion factor will work with? <u>**Oh yes!!**</u>

Grant Jeffrey also applied this conversion factor to Ezekiel's 430 years. Jeffery subtracted the 70 years of captivity (time served) from the total sin of 430 years and considered the remainder (360 years) as "parole" or probation. Jeffrey notes that the returning Jews still did not let the **land** lay fallow for Sabbath **rests**. Therefore he applied Leviticus 26:18 (where the Lord says "If after all this you will not listen to me, I will punish you for your sins seven times over") to the remaining 360 years and determined a residual penalty of 2520 prophetic years. (360 x 7 = 2520) Converting this according to Anderson's adjustment we get 2483 total actual years of penalty remaining (after the 70 years served). Applying this to 536 BC, we get 1948 AD (remember there was no year "zero") when God finally returned the Israelite nation to the **land**. The total captivity was served. This was a precise fulfillment that also satisfied Isaiah 66:7,8. "Can a nation be born in just one day?" Yes! The United Nations took a vote "one day" and Israel was reborn.

We have to pause at the deep significance of this discovery. Israel was on probation 2,483 years. **Almost all of Western history!!**

From the rise of Greece and the rise and fall of Rome, through the Middle Ages, the Renaissance and the Reformation, until the "fullness of time." This includes the entire Christian era - and all of the "the church" and the world's feeble attempts through the crusades and the "protectorate" campaigns to re-establish the Holy Lands as a national homeland for the Jews. Theologians of the Middle Ages (and the Reformation) were puzzled by the Scripture's continual reference to "Israel". Who was this "Israel" God was speaking about when there was no "Israel" - the nation of Israel vanished in 70 AD. So these "theologians" solved the problem with their flesh. They made up an answer rather than waiting on the Lord and trusting the Word - being at **rest** about such things.

Man went in "logical" circles to explain how Biblical "Israel" was really "the Church". All the while, God had the very day and hour of birth pains already selected - for He has an appointment (Mo`ed) with Israel.

And these "birth pains" as Jesus calls them, World War I and World War II, showed us clearly the capability for evil and destruction man can embrace in his quest for a solution to the question of two thousand years "who is Israel?" Satan killed over 6 million Jews in six years but Israel was reborn - and repopulated - exactly as God had foretold.

All of Western history and all of government and foreign policy has been shaped by the Creator in the crucible of "time" to bring forth again, a land for His children, Israel, right on schedule. How exact was this "schedule"? See Appendix

A1 – Error Analysis.

Today we have the Nation of Israel - and we have seen dozens of prophecies concerning that land come to pass.

[Note: Concerning the prophesies of Table 9-1: It is left as an exercise to the reader to determine which "return" of Israel God is referring to: Post-exilic, post-Diaspora, or post-tribulation - or perhaps all three?]

Deuteronomy	30:3	Psalm	126:1
Isaiah	1:26	Ezekiel	16:55
	10:21		
	51:11	Hosea	3:5
Jeremiah	12:15		14:7
	16:15		
	24:6	Joel	2:25
	27:22		3:1
	29.10		
	29:14	Amos	9:14
	30:3		
	30:10	Obadiah	:15
	30:18		
	31:4	Micah	5:3
	31:8		
	31:16	Zephaniah	3:20
	32:15	Zechariah	2:12
	32:37		10:6
	42:12		

Table 9A-1 (repeated)
PROPHECIES OF ISRAEL'S RETURN

Is the existence of Israel assured in Heaven? Has she not triumphed smartly against all her foes in every conflict? The Six Day War (the name alone tells you how that one went) saw the return of the West Bank to Israel and the reclaiming of Jerusalem (Praise God!). The Yom Kippur War saw the resolve of the people who were stunned by a sneak attack on the holiest of days. They overcame superior numbers and again won more land for Israel. And just a few years ago, in the Persian Gulf War we saw the miracle of harmless missiles. You may remember that Saddam Hussein launched forty Scud missiles at Israel during the first months of 1991. While the nations of the world watched by television, the haters of God thrashed out against the rule of God and His Word. Tell me, how many Jewish citizens were killed by those 40 missiles of hate? NOT

ONE! Despite great fear and some urban panic, not one Israeli death was directly attributed to the Scud missile blasts. Considerable damage was suffered as these weapons, meant for mass destruction, fell on the cities of Israel, but a God of mercy did not let these arrows from hell touch even one of His children - [Praise God!].

Besides the existence of the nation of Israel and the global preaching of the Gospel (which are absolute confirmations that we are in the last days), are there other warning flags?

9B   WARNING FLAGS

Are there any Scriptural warning signs that these are the last days? Oh yes - let's just take a quick peek at a few prophecies.

Daniel 12:4: "Many will go here and there to increase knowledge."

100 years ago, if you had any traveling to do, you walked, sailed or rode on a farm animal. From the time of Daniel (ca 500 BC) until this century, the variations in mechanisms for human wanderings have not changed. Stop for just a minute and consider this - it is incredible! Until the 20th century, you traveled from city to city by foot or hoof or sail. The same choices Adam or Noah had! [Note: The exception to this statement is rail travel. Although limited to a few inter-urban corridors, rail was a choice in the last half of the 19th century - but only available in the most developed commercial areas. The rest of the world still walked!]

When you realize how "new" the options of bicycle, motorcycle, truck, auto and aircraft are, you get a better perspective on Daniel's prophecy. Travel speeds went from 20 miles a day to 60 miles per hour to 600 miles per hour, almost overnight. Is this what Daniel spoke of?

Knowledge will increase - well, so it seems. We have experts on every aspect of life and living. Consider this: of all the scientists who ever lived throughout all time - 90% are alive today!

How about one-world government? Since the League of Nations at the end of World War I through the United Nations today, we have squeezed the concept of "national sovereignty" into a myopic petri dish that is labeled "New

World Order."

We organize global commerce according to the G-7 (The loose federation of major economic powers, including the USA, Japan, Germany, Great Britain, etc.), we organize justice according to the Hague World court and exercise only politically acceptable technology (ozone hole, global warming, toxic waste, local marine harvesting, etc., etc.).

Of all these prophesied attendants of life in the last days, the most obsessive is the global pursuit of a Middle East peace. A peace not by acculturation and love, but peace by <u>treaty</u> - peace by legislation - peace by covenant. [Not a "peace", but a "piece" of paper!]

We give headlines to those who organize peace talks. We give prizes to those who develop treaties. We've changed our economy and our culture to force-fit this issue into "our time."

Does anyone read Scripture?

Have any of these "world leaders" noticed that the 70th week of Daniel begins with this very covenant of man-made peace - a treaty of evil and deceit between Satanic global forces and the blinded children of God's Israel? Why is America leading this "sign-now" solution? What a cherished headline we pursue - "World Ends at Camp David."

If you doubt the accuracy of any of the other prophetic venues described in this work - please follow the crowd in its madness to force (coerce, cajole) Israel and the Arab world into a man-made peace.

When you combine these obsessions with other recent history, you see the necessary pieces fall into place. Moslem countries once part of the Soviet Union, are now free - and very violent. Hundreds of nuclear weapons are no longer under Moscow's control - and the money to buy weapons and delivery systems is already in the hands of oil rich Arabs.

Ask yourself what the chances were in 500 BC for Ezekiel to properly envision a union of Libya and Syria and Egypt and Iraq/Iran (Ezekiel 38). Why Libya? North Africa did not fall to the Islamic hordes until the 8th Century AD (over 12 centuries after Ezekiel was dead!)But he saw Libya as part of the force against Israel. And we have all seen the pictures of Muammar Qaddafi awarding medals to terrorists who machine-gunned Jewish school buses - heroes for sure.

We cannot appreciate the alignment of the nations today without a clear understanding of the God-hating forces of prehistory. Do your best to follow the development of this "last battle" as we build the array from ancient days to capture the Big Picture. We need to see "time" God's way - and we need to look where He tells us to look - at the big chunks He calls out as:

430-480-430!

This message of 430-480-430 will be examined in chapter 12. But first we must understand the message of the unknown day and hour.

10.0 KNOWING THE DAY AND THE HOUR

Our Lord wore "many hats" during His first advent, His first visit to earth as Jesus the Christ, the Messiah of God. That is to say that He wore the garments of and therefore led the life of many prophetic images of the "Anointed One." We see Him clearly as the suffering servant of Isaiah 53 and the Book of Hebrews tells us He is our High Priest who lives to intercede for us continually. [Thank you Jesus!]. In Zechariah 6:13 we see Him as the union of King and Priest, a role reserved to God alone since He is our rightful King. We also see Jesus as the Son of God/teacher/master/shepherd and in John 14:2 we see Him as the Bride Groom who leaves "...*to prepare a place for you.*"

With all of this in mind when we study the words and see Jesus speaking as the 2nd person of the Godhead, does it matter which hat He is wearing at the time or who His audience might be? Do these variables affect the interpretation of the passage? Yes, surely.

When Jesus says to the woman caught in the act of adultery: *"Where are thy accusers?"* and then adds: *"Neither do I accuse thee!"* Or when Jesus says to the paralytic: *"Have faith - thy sins are forgiven thee."* This is surely a different voice, a different Jesus from the Son of Man who says to another sinner: *"Depart from me you worker of iniquity. I never knew you!!!"*

So when Jesus tells His Disciples that:

> *"No one knows about that day or hour, not even the angels in heaven, nor the Son, but only the Father"*

Matthew 24:36, with which **voice** is He speaking?

He certainly isn't saying that as God, the second person of the Trinity, He doesn't know the answer! The reference to "the Son" is a direct reference to "obedience." As the obedient servant of God, He, Jesus, has no need in His current walk (first advent) to have such information - He is content to trust in God (the Father) completely - and **rest** in the assurance that God has everything under control and that His (Jesus') future is "determined" in God's Holy Will to be whatever is best.

[NOTE: The phrase "not the Son" does not appear in the oldest and most reliable manuscripts - <u>but</u> - even if it should be included, it does not affect the role of Jesus as the Son of God - the person of the Son is obedient and therefore does not need to know - only to obey. As Jesus Himself tells us:

"I say what I have heard / what I have seen - "]

It is not His place (as the Son) to <u>initiate</u> action on His own - but rather to be obedient to and in the center of the Will of the Father. As conveyed to Him by the Holy Spirit the prayer He teaches us has as its first petition that:

"Thy Will be done"

and in the Garden of Gethsemane only a few days hence, Jesus says again:

"Not my Will but Thine be done."

So when Jesus says "no man knows," does that mean no man will ever know? This certainly has been the position of interpretations through out the centuries (i.e. that the return of Jesus will be a complete surprise). Jesus says: *"Therefore keep watch, because you do not know on what day **your Lord** will come."* Matthew 24:42 And again He says: *"..the son of man will come at an hour when you do not expect Him."* Luke 12:40.

If we honor these statements as truth (which they are) how can any believer (this author included) have the tenacity, the reckless, the almost blasphemous abandon to indicate a time for Jesus' return? That Jesus may return at any time, at any moment, is a standard and universally accepted teaching in the Church. No one knows when. This truth is called the 'Doctrine of Immanence'. This work **does not** challenge that teaching. We will show that this teaching specifically pertains to the Lord's return for His Bride. Furthermore, what also will be shown in this work is that when wearing His Crown (a special hat - when fulfilling the will of the Father as regards the Messiah and King of Israel), Jesus' return into time **is known** and preparations for the second visitation should be undertaken (**TODAY!**).

Well, let's consider other Scriptures and then let's reconsider with what "voice" (or in what capacity) Jesus was speaking - and to whom He was speaking.

First, let's look at some "apparent contradictions" in the promises of God and see if we can gain some insight into the mind of the Absolute.

This is the right and proper thing to do for God says through Isaiah 1:18:

"Come now let us reason together..."

[But He also warns that we might not get very far. . .because Isaiah 55:8,9 says:

"For my thoughts are not your thoughts, neither are

your ways my ways, declares the Lord.

As the heavens are higher than the earth so are my ways

higher than your ways and my thoughts than your

thoughts"]

We will look at four examples in the Word and try to gain some insight into the perfect mind of God.

1. Consider Jonah's message to the people of Nineveh:

    "Forty more days and Nineveh will be destroyed." (Jonah 3:4)

But forty days passed and Nineveh **was not** overturned. This bothered the rebellious prophet very much and he was angry with God. He probably felt like he'd been "used" by God and made to look like a "fool" . But is this what happened? **NO!** A miracle is what happened! The power of God's Word touched the hearts of the people of Nineveh and they <u>repented</u> - therefore God spared them. Jonah should have been joyful, but he did not understand the mind of God. Oh, he understood <u>some</u> of the nature of God for he says:

"I knew that you are a gracious and compassionate

God, slow to anger and abounding in love, a God who

<u>*relents*</u> *from sending calamity."* (Jonah 4:2)

What value does God place on "repentance" ? <u>Infinite</u> value! Beyond our understanding! For repentance is a demonstration of love through obedience - a free will offering of the spirit of the man (or woman). And for love to be real it <u>must</u> be freely given. If you think real love is easy then why is it so hard to say, "I'm wrong" or "I'm sorry"? When it actually hurts our pride (which is fallen) - then it'sreal.   And so it was with the people of Nineveh - **the people believed God** ...**and repented!!**

Was God's Word a lie?   No!   The city was "overturned" (NIV) or "overthrown" (KJV). From the King to the lowliest shepherd, the Ninevites fasted and humbled themselves before God. They repented of their violence and evil ways. They prayed (in sackcloth and ashes) and worshipped God their creator. Forty days later, all the people had new hearts and new values and new ways of doing things. They had "turned over" a new leaf! The <u>old ways</u> were "overthrown" and they gave glory to God with their spirits. Thus a gracious, merciful and compassionate Sovereign Lord spared them their just punishment.

2. How about Isaiah's message from God to Hezekiah:
"This is what the Lord says: Put your house in order, because you are going to die; you will not recover." (Isaiah 38:1).
How did Hezekiah respond?

He wept bitterly! (Not tears of feeling sorry for one's self and arguing with God, but tears of repentance - knowing and seeing the shortcomings of his "walk".)

What did God do in response to Hezekiah's repentance? God's response was to add 15 years to Hezekiah's life and to defend Hezekiah from his enemies.

Was God's Word a lie? **No!** Hezekiah did die - his spirit died to self - died to pride - "it never recovered". We too are blessed this way. We are to reckon our old self crucified with Christ - dead to sin. Can we take the step Hezekiah took?

"Though He slay me
Yet shall I trust in Him! (Job 13:15) (KJV)

3. Then there is God's covenant to His chosen people that the land, the land given through an unconditional covenant to Abraham , would be theirs <u>forever</u>. Then God went and took the land away by foreign military conquest and sent the people into captivity. Did God Lie? **OH, NO!** As Paul says *"God Forbid!"* and again - *"Let God be true, and every man a liar!"* (Romans 3:4)(KJV)

God said to His chosen:

"I will be your God and You will be my people." (Jeremiah 7:23)

But the descendants of Jacob forsook the covenant and therefore the blessing - the peace (**rest**) of Jesus.

They freely chose not to have God as their first love but to worship strange gods - idols - the things of this world - the trappings of Egypt. They also freely chose not to be God's people - but rather to be people of the world and therefore they became children of the ruler of this world.

They broke the covenant and received the due penalty of their ways. Yet, God still brought back a remnant, a handful of believers, and tried again.

Today, we believers in the Blood of Jesus cannot arrogantly accept the gift of salvation as a fire insurance policy on damnation. "Belief" is a state of mind and heart that is exhibited by our actions. ("Faith without works is dead also." James 2:26b (KJV))

Jesus tells the Jews that the owner of the vineyard will destroy the current tenants and give the land over to new tenants - THAT'S US!!! (Praise God!) But Paul reminds us that we were grafted in and therefore we can be just as easily grafted out - live your faith or loose it! Act like an adopted son of God!

4. Note the precise words of Isaiah 32:14,15 as God speaks concerning the destruction of Israel and Jerusalem:

> 14: *"The fortress will be abandoned, the noisy city deserted; citadel and watchtower will become a wasteland **forever**, the delight of donkeys, a pasture for flocks,*
>
> 15: *till (**until**) the Spirit is poured upon us from on high, and the desert becomes a fertile field and the fertile field seems like a forest!"*

Forever. . . until? What kind of concept is this? To our mind "forever" is an absolute that has no end. But we live in time and forget about the One who created time – the transcendent One who sees all time at once. For Him, "time" is just another element of creation that is subject to His Will. Therefore, the **forever/until** oxymoron is wholly consistent with the God who issues decrees from "eternity" (a place outside of 'time').

What a problem it must have been for the theologians of the Middle Ages, the Renaissance and the Reformation to understand who and what "Israel" was and how to interpret the prophecies concerning Israel, especially when it was clear to everyone that the nation of Israel was not!

> *"By faith we understand that the universe was formed at God's command, so that what is seen was not made out of what was visible."* Hebrews 11:3

So we are reminded that *"...with God all things are possible"* [even apparent contradictions] and

> *"You are in error because you do not know the Scriptures or the power of God."* (Matthew 22:29)

Back to our apparent conflict. How can Jesus say, *"no man knoweth the day or the hour"* yet this text will imply otherwise.

Let's look at Judgment. (Even though this is not a pleasant subject, it must be done.) When God spoke to Ninevah, it was in judgment; but this judgment was <u>staved off by repentance</u>. When God speaks of the tribulation, He speaks of judgment (wrath) on the world - **not** staved off by repentance.

When I became a Christian (Thank you Father!!) and first read the Revelation, I was amazed - astounded - that the victims of God's wrath <u>would not repent</u>. I was confounded that Satan would persist unto inevitable defeat and not repent. Only pure pride could be so stubborn! [I've yet to understand evil (and hate and pride) in its <u>fullest</u> abomination (and I'm glad that I don't), but I praise and thank God that I have been saved by the blood of Jesus (the very image and essence of mercy) and also spared that vision of ultimate perdition.]

God's wrath is well documented throughout Scripture as the great and terrible day of the Lord. References abound. Those who become the objects of destruction cannot say they were not warned. The events of this tribulation are also well documented. There is a 7-year timetable - a schedule of events - and a precision of execution down to the day and hour (and I personally believe down to the minute and second and micro-second, etc.!!!). How can the people who see:

A. The edict ending the daily sacrifice not know that it is but 1290 days until the Anti-Christ commits the abomination of desolation? (See Daniel 12:11) and

B. That from the signing of the covenant with the Anti-Christ, there will be but 7 years (Daniel 9:27).

C. Those people who see "A" and "B" are **not** the children of repentance.

To those who <u>knew</u> and <u>repented</u>, God will show mercy. At the time of the great flood there were believers and they were protected. Noah and his family had 120 years of general revelation (Genesis 6:3) in which God provided time to build the Ark and 7 days of specific revelation (Genesis 7:4) to prepare for the coming voyage (flood).

Moses and the Jews had general revelation about the death of the first-born of Pharaoh (Exodus 4:21-23) and they had at least four days of specific revelation of the Passover plague (Exodus 12:3) that would bring this death.

The issue here is that God announced what He would do beforehand and **also** provided for the protection and well-being of His children (believers and their families). [But note: To be saved, the Old Testament believers had to remain <u>inside</u> (inside their house, inside the Ark) to be protected. Likewise, we must reside **(rest)** in Christ.] These events, the flood and the Passover, occurred at an appointed (Mo`ed: Hebrew set time) time - set down before-hand in eternity. And I believe this is also true with the wrath of God and the Judgments of the Tribulation. They are also "appointed" for a **set time**.

But Paul, who well understood the "appointed" feasts and their fulfillment in the Christ, tells us... "For God did not "appoint" us to suffer wrath...."
(I Thessalonians 5:9a)

We, the believers, the very body of Christ, are not destined to be objects of God's wrath - and that is the key to understanding the "apparent contradiction" in knowing the day and the hour.

It is the <u>wrath</u> and <u>judgment</u> that are <u>appointed</u>. They are appointed for a **set time**, foretold and demonstrated in the feasts and accomplished in and through Christ Jesus. The believers (those who repent) are **not part** of this appointment.

Hence, for us there is **no set time**. The church is a mystery of God's salvation to the Gentiles (Praise God!!). This salvation is a gift and God will not take His gift back. (Romans 11:29)

But the feasts - the feasts are picture-perfect prophecy. The feasts will be fulfilled - as appointed - according to **set time**. Jesus' role in these feasts provides the fulfillment. So as Jesus came the first time not to destroy the Law but to fulfill it, so too with the second coming Jesus will apply the Law - and this is the area of confusion. We are not under Law (Romans 6:14b), neither are we appointed to wrath.

If we are not appointed (Mo`ed) to wrath, then just where will God's believers be when the 7 years of wrath (the Tribulation) are prosecuted on the world?

Well, we won't be here!

How this will happen and when this miraculous intervention of God's Holy Spirit for our protection (shield) will occur is quite unknown - and hotly debated. I speak of the Rapture of the church.

Look carefully at Matthew 25:1-13. This is the parable of the ten virgins - Jesus delivers this parable **immediately after** the dissertation on the unknown hour (Matthew 24:36-51). The parable begins with the words, *"At that time the kingdom of heaven will be like ..."* . *"Then shall the kingdom of heaven be likened... "(KJV)*

When Jesus is speaking about the "unknown hour", He is talking about when - as the Bridegroom - He (Jesus) is going to return to claim his Bride. This is the "voice" He speaks with here. Not with the Voice of the commander of God's army or the Voice of One who will sit in Judgment, but rather the Voice of love, the Voice of our betrothed - who promises once again to return for His virgin bride - *"so that where I am, there ye may be also!!"* (John 14:3) (KJV)

These words of Jesus begin with a phrase taken from Jewish tradition regarding the wedding preparation - "I go to prepare a place for you." To understand the "voice" we need a little insight into the customs of the First Century BC. After the bride's father accepted the groom's dowry, the groom left their house and went to build a house of his own...a house for the bride. When the bridegroom was asked (as he labored on this new home), "When is the wedding?" He would answer "ask my Father" for it was the Father's responsibility and prerogative to determine the readiness of the marriage dwelling…. to determine when the house was finished.

So we have an interesting conflict resolved. The Second Coming of Jesus as the Commander, Only-Son, High Priest, Judge and King, **is appointed** (and I believe discoverable from the prophecies of Scripture). "I make known the end from the beginning." (Isaiah 46:10) But the coming of the Bridegroom to claim His Bride, "The dew of his youth," **is not known**….except to the Father.

So the church and the church-age enter Scripture as a mystery and depart from the scene as a mystery. And this is rightly so, for Jesus tells Nicodemus:

> *"The wind blows wherever it pleases. You hear its sound but you cannot tell where it comes from or where it is going. So it is with everyone born of the Spirit."* (John 3:8)

Because we are born of the Spirit, we are subject to the laws of the Spirit *"in order that God's purpose in election might stand!"* (Romans 9:11c) therefore we will be **gone with the wind**…carried away by the **SPIRIT**.

If this insight into the wedding tradition is not enough to convince you, look carefully at Matthew 24:42. Please note Jesus' self reference as "your Lord". He is clearly speaking to Believers, people who have Jesus in their hearts as "Lord" [He is clearly not speaking to the unrepentant, even though He is their Lord also…"*For every knee shall bow…*"]

It is as "your Lord" that Jesus ("your Master, your Husband") comes to fetch the Bride. The day and hour that is unknown is the time of the Rapture.

11.0 WHEN IS THE RAPTURE?

[Note: As we have shown in chapter 10, it is the Rapture that Jesus places at an "unknown" hour - part of the mystery of the church. Even to speculate on when this might occur seems somewhat distrustful - but such speculation is common within the body. Forgive us Lord for this curiosity and help us to be ready! Kum ba yah!! MARANATHA!!!]

There are three prevailing theories of when the blesséd event – the Rapture of the church – might occur:

1. Before the Tribulation (pre-Trib)
2. During the Tribulation (mid-Trib)
3. After the Tribulation (post-Trib)

That surely seems to cover all of the possibilities – or does it? No teacher of Jesus' day would have foreseen that God would "expand time" so that the 69th week of Daniel would be separated from the 70th week of Daniel (the Tribulation) by some 2,000 years. This was truly a mystery - the mystery of the church, the body of Christ. (See Colossians 1:24-26.) Many of the believers in the first century church (who were initially all Jewish) looked for the return of the Messiah in their day. They thought the 70th week would immediately follow the 69th week. But the 70th and final week still has not come. Even with the prophecies described in this text [which I believe show the proper time frame for the 70th week] is there any hint of another dispensation – another time-expansion for yet another mystery of God to be interjected between the ages. But God **IS** sovereign and will do all that pleases Him! So, assuming that such an undeclared new age does not occur (there being no evidence for it yet interpreted), then the three choices given above still stand - either a pre-, mid- or post-Tribulation Rapture.

The Rapture of the church is the event spoken of by Paul in 1 Thessalonians 4:13-18:

> *"But I would not have you to be ignorant, brethren, concerning them which are asleep, that ye sorrow not,*

> *even as others which have no hope. For if we believe that Jesus died and rose again, even so them also which sleep in Jesus will God bring with him. For this we say unto you by the word of the Lord, that we which are alive and remain unto the coming of the Lord shall not precede them which are asleep. For the Lord himself shall descend from heaven with a shout, with the voice of the archangel, and with the trump of God: and the dead in Christ shall rise first: Then we which are alive and remain shall be caught up together with them in the clouds, to meet the Lord in the air: and so shall we ever be with the Lord. Wherefore comfort one another with these words."* KJV

So we see all of those who are "in Christ" taken from the earth to be with Jesus. It is assumed by most commentators that this is a very quick event, for Paul also says in 1 Corinthians 15:51,52: *"Behold, I shew you a mystery; We shall not all sleep, but we shall all be changed, In a moment, in the twinkling of an eye, at the last trump: for the trumpet shall sound, and the dead shall be raised incorruptible, and we shall be changed."* KJV

The reason there are difficulties placing those events or this event in time is the question of Tribulation believers and "wrath." What happens to the people who come to salvation during the Tribulation?

If the Rapture is before the wrath (pre-Trib), what happens to the Gentiles and Jews who come to Jesus <u>after</u> the Rapture (i.e. during the Tribulation)? Do they have to "suffer wrath" because they came to the party late? Do they miss the wedding feast? (NOTE: This question could be tossed away by supposing there won't be any more believers saved during the Tribulation.) The 144,000 sealed believing Jews who remain during the Tribulation will be protected for 1260 days (see Revelation 12:6), but the souls of believers (those who washed their robes in the blood of the Lamb - Revelation 7:14) killed during the Tribulation **are seen** by John in heaven during this 7-year period. HELP! If the church is Raptured and the Jews protected, who, then, are those martyred true believers? Where do they come from?

The very same arguments apply if the Rapture is mid-Trib with the additional difficulty of wrath. The 7 bowls of God's wrath are poured out upon the earth but since "we are not appointed to wrath", this seems to indicate that our presence is not required.

And finally, for the post-Trib variation, the argument of wrath persists: Why would God have believers go through this awful time? There is an exception to the wrath problem for the believing Jew. They are like the Jews of Exodus who were separated from the Egyptians. The believing Jews lived in Goshen – away from the evil of Egypt, the world and its ways. This 'separated' living kept them safe from the plagues.

When the plagues struck Egypt, Goshen was spared – no lice, no frogs, no locusts, no hail, no darkness – leave Goshen at your own risk. In the Tribulation, God removes the believing Jews to a "place in the desert" where they are spared.

It may be that, like the Jews who passed through the Red Sea, so the believing remnant who are left will be the fulfillment of Psalm 91:7. Great devastation will be to the left and to the right but it will not come near them. But again, where do the martyrs of Revelation 7 come from? Do they miss the wedding feast?

The issues are complex and the details seem lost in the noise of battle. These questions are **way** beyond the scope of this text. There is, however, one easy answer to all these questions. God, who loves us beyond our understanding, who died to set us free (from the way of sin and death – yes – but free from worry too), has my best interest and your best interests at the center of His heart. So let us **rest** our minds and hearts in Him who is faithful.

What is apparent is that the 70th week of Daniel, which is called the "time of Jacob's trouble" by the Old Testament and "the Great Tribulation" by the New Testament, is a period reserved for God and Israel. **This is a <u>Jewish</u> 7 years.** By trial and tribulation, God will finally bring Israel to repentance and therefore to redemption. During this period both the believers and the pagans will suffer. First the believers will suffer the <u>wrath of Satan</u> and then the pagans will sufffer the <u>wrath of God</u>. The Church has no appointment (Mo`ed) with God's wrath (See I Thessalonians 5:9) - the rebellious do. Protect us, Holy Father!

<u>Three Audiences:</u>

A careful comparison of the Gospel references to the end of the age (Matthew 24, Mark 13 and Luke 17 and 21) will show that Jesus addresses three different audiences:

1.   First there is the audience of the nation of Israel and the believers who were alive (this included those believers who were with Him at that time).

They would see and suffer great distress. They would see Jerusalem destroyed and the Temple torn down, not one stone left upon another.

The order of events in Luke 21 is quite clear. Verses 8-11 are a snapshot of the history of the Christian age: war after war [which is how we study "history" in school!], earthquakes, famines, pestilence and fearful events. Then (after all this "history") there will be "great signs from heaven."

Note Verse 12 begins with:

*"But **before** all this....."*

that is before the "history" (events) of the Christian age "... you, (those I speak to now and all the people of Israel...He who has ears let him hear), will suffer." And this suffering includes the destruction of Jerusalem and therefore the nation (people) of Israel also, for in Verse 24 He says:

> *"They will fall by the sword and will be taken as prisoners to all the nations."*

The Jews would be spread across the face of the whole earth and Jerusalem would be trampled.

They (Jesus' Disciples) would suffer humiliation, hatred, imprisonment and death on account of their love for His Name. But do not be troubled, they are told, for first the Gospel must be preached to all nations.

Many of those men and women who heard Jesus' message knew how large the world was. The Greeks of 400 BC had estimated the size of the earth (globe) at about 8,000 miles in diameter. If this physical size was lost to them, they understood that it was a long journey to Tarshish or Dedan. Caesar had reached England in 58 BC and Alexander had reached India in 330 BC. The Disciples were well aware that it was going to take more than seven years to preach the good news to all those folks between England and India!

2.   The second audience that Jesus addresses is the born again

believers – you and I – who will stand guard and carry the gospel to the ends of the earth. We are the generation of the birth pains. We are to fill our lamps with oil and be ready. Be ready for what? For the day and the hour that is <u>unknown</u>. Jesus speaks about the "day and hour" in Luke 12, Mark 13 and Matthew 24, 25.

It is very important that the reader take note of the structure and presentation of the "end of age" discourses. Luke 17 is the prophecy of the "end of the age", but the warning to be ready is given in Luke 12. All of Chapter 12 is devoted to being **separate** – forsaking the things of this world – forsaking even life itself in return for the life that Christ promises us in His Kingdom. Be ready, for He is coming. He is coming "<u>from</u>" a wedding feast (see Luke 12:36). The feast is not over, <u>it is waiting</u>, it is prepared for believers! Jesus is coming <u>from</u> the feast (preparations) **to get the bride** and bring the bride to that feast so that He might serve her. Their time of faithful service is over, now the Groom will serve them! (Praise God!).

This parable has nothing to do with the wrath/judgment component associated with the end of the age. Luke properly puts it after the message on worry, because we are to **rest** without worry, assured that Jesus' return (for us) is for the purpose of the wedding feast, oneness and celebration.

In Mark 13 and in Matthew 24, the admonition to be ready is <u>appended</u> to the end of the age discourses. These admonitions are clearly "<u>second thoughts</u>". The "end of age" prophecy discourse <u>terminates</u> in each gospel with Jesus' powerful declaration that:

> "*Heaven and earth will pass away*
>
> *but my words will never pass away.*"
>
> (Matthew 24:35 and Mark 13:31)
>
> -- FINIS! --

The "day and hour" reminder <u>is added</u> to or tacked on the end of the wrath/judgment sequences by the inspired authors to remind and comfort <u>believers</u> that they **are not** the focus of God's wrath, but rather the objects of His love (a marriage love).

Both Mark and Matthew use the master of the house parable. For the returning Master has come to take His obedient servants from the earthly abode where they have served in faithfulness to the heavenly home prepared <u>in the Kingdom</u>. ("*I go to prepare a place for you.*" John 14:2b KJV).

This is made especially clear-cut in Matthew 25 when Jesus **immediately** augments the day/hour admonition with the parable of the ten virgins. Here comes the bridegroom – are you ready? It's time to go!

The second audience therefore is "the Church" the Body of Christ, and we must be ready to go. ["Your Lord" is coming - not the judge 'n' jury!]

But we don't know when. It is a mystery as the church is a mystery. But for the appointed (Mo`ed) judgment, this **time is set** (as the feasts are set) and I believe it is also revealed in Scripture.

3. The third audience is the Nation of Israel at the time of Judgment. Remember that the Jews would be spread across the face of the whole earth and Jerusalem would be trampled.

How long?

...until the times of the Gentiles are fulfilled.

How long is that?

We will look at the prophecy of Hosea and calculate this duration in Chapter 13. But first, let's look again at Luke 21 (and Mark 13 and Matthew 24).This third audience is specifically the believing Jewish remnant that is sealed in the Revelation.

"You will only observe with your eyes
and see the punishment of the wicked" Psalm 91:8

These believers will be kept secure in prophetic Goshen, that "place in the desert", where the Holy Spirit will protect them. (Separated…at last!) (More on this miracle of faith in Chapter 15.)

With the believers "removed", God's wrath comes on the earth unexpectedly – like in the days of Noah. The people of Noah's day were warned, but would not repent. So it will be again. Those who laugh at God will be left to experience His wine press.

And **then**, after the great Diaspora and the age of the Gentiles, **then** after the days of the abomination that causes desolation, **then** after unequaled distress, **then** there will be signs in the Sun and Moon and stars (Luke 21:25).

Those who are "watching" (those protected by God and resting in Jesus with all their heart) will see these signs and they will see the Son of Man coming in Glory - and so will the rest of the world. But this group of believers still has a job to do!

"*When these things **begin** to take place, stand up and lift up your heads*

(i.e. rejoice!!!) *Because your redemption is drawing near!*" (Luke 21:28) Praise God!

But before all this, there needs to be an Israel that is a Jewish nation, a Jerusalem that is a Jewish city and a Temple for Satan to disgrace and pollute.

We have seen two of these three requirements met in our lifetimes – Praise God!

12.0 THE BIG PICTURE 430-480-430

We are going to follow the progress of Israel from Egyptian captivity to Babylonian captivity. During this sojourn, Israel was commanded by God to cleanse themselves from evil:

"Be Holy because I am Holy"

But the people failed to heed this divine directive.

The people are ordered to cleanse the land and to live "separate" Holy lives, consecrated to God. But again they fail. Eventually, God Himself will cleanse the nation and the land via the Babylonian captivity. But this event is only prophecy ----- for the final cleansing has yet to take place. God will eventually take charge and perform both cleansing tasks Himself:

a) He will cleanse the nation spiritually with His own blood; and,

b) He will cleanse the nation and the land physically during the tribulation.

All of the events in Israel's history are pointers and prophecy to these events.

The prophetic nature of Israel's history is not merely poetic or symbolic. This 'history' exhibits **unparalleled exactness**. Through seemingly random events God clearly demonstrates His transcendence of time and His total Sovereignty over all creation. What we call "the past" is a **precise** reflection of "tomorrow".

We tend to think of history as a connected chain — a cause and effect sequential process that is "free running." Such a view would not portray history as having a geometric structure. Neither would such a classical view see within this veiled structure choreographed events and prophetic time tables for future "history."

But God controls history. It should not surprise us that seemingly unrelated events fit together in a pattern as beautiful as a "random" snow flake. History is an orchestrated picture painted by God to reflect and glorify His Name. All creation is so arranged [the stars, for example, tell the story of Jesus (see D. J. Kennedy *The Christian Zodiac*)].

God has set a major prophetic "time stone" in the history of Israel. It is a period of formative revelation broken into three major blocks of 430-480-430 years. See Figure 12-1.

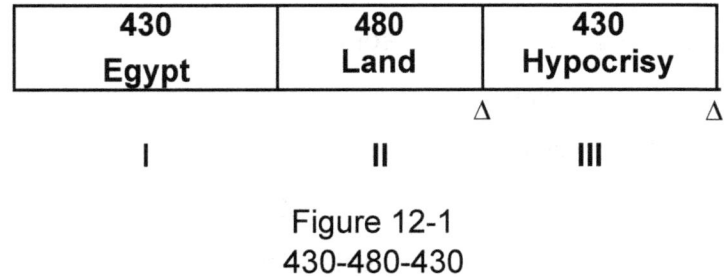

Figure 12-1
430-480-430

Exodus 12:40-41 tells us that 430 years was the time in Egypt *to the very day*. I Kings 6 tells us the first Temple was 480 years from the Exodus and the prophet Ezekiel tells his people that their sin is 430 years (see Ezekiel 4). We will show that this 430 years was spiritually distributed across the whole nation and physically represented by the precise time between the Temples (shown by the triangles in Figure 12-1).

The Scripture is replete with the use of round numbers. Numbers like 10, 40, 70 are quite common. And there are some instances where poetic approximations can be inferred. But numbers like 430, 480 and 430 again, linked one behind the other, should say to even the casual observer, "Hey, look at me! I'm too unusual to just be happenstance."

The Lord told Ezekiel that the sin of the House of Israel was 390 years and the sin of the House of Judah was 40 years [so that the sin of the whole nation was 430 years]. (Ezekiel 4) What is God really saying?

I believe the Lord is saying something like this:

"I redeemed you out of Egypt and gave you your own land. You are to be *DIFFERENT* from other people.

"I gave you the Law, the Torah, and I even dwelt in your man-made Temple. My Name and My Glory are with you, but you are not with me!

"You want to be just like everybody else — worshipping the gods of this earth — rather than consecrated to me."

"Your 430 years of Temple worship were no different (in your heart) than your 430 years of paganism in Egypt. Therefore you (and your worship) are hypocrisy and your Temple is hypocrisy, **BOTH MUST GO** from my Holy land and the land must be purified.

For God to take such a drastic action and dispossess His own children from their inheritance (given by covenant through Abraham) something had to be seriously wrong. We had better get the message and clearly understand the Holy context.

Let's add some more detail to the Big Picture. See Figure 12-2.

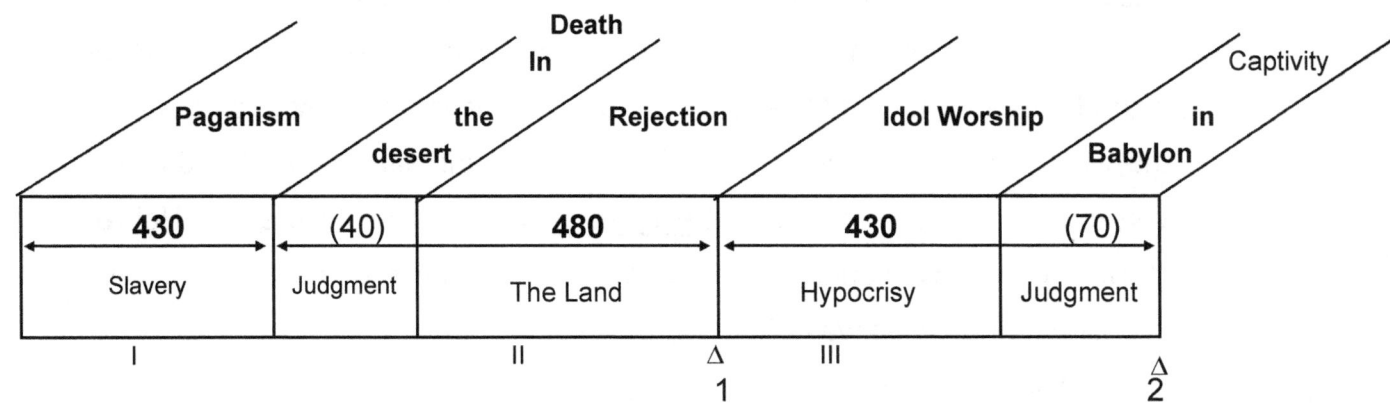

Figure 12-2
THE TWO JUDGMENTS

We've made the graphic take on a bit more detail and an additional dimension. Now let's follow the journey of Israel to the Promised Land. We see that the trip to Babylon began with the 40 years in the desert. The hardened hearts of the Redeemed Israelites remained stubborn and God let them die in the desert [Note: He cleansed His people <u>first</u>, then He set about cleansing the land]. So the trip to the "Kingdom" starts in Judgment. No, that's not exactly true; the trip started in <u>awe</u> and <u>fear</u> of God but degenerated quickly into complaining. It then progressed to disobedience (to the Sabbath and the Manna) and then finally decomposed into outright rebellion by rejecting God's offer of the land. The people refused to enter the land because there were giants in the Land! These "giants" were really in their hearts - an entrenched desire for sinful living. That act of rejection sealed the Judgment. Had the hearts of the Jews been right, the next step would have been to clean house in The Holy Land, but that was put on hold for 40 years. First, God had to clean house in Israel. [This cleansing period has not yet ended, as we shall see.]

With the death of Moses and the rest of the Jews (20 years of age and over), God took His only two remaining witnesses of that generation, Caleb and Joshua, and started into the land.

Now Joshua (the oldest Hebrew left) is the leader and he was given the job of cleansing the land. Hard as he tried, Joshua could not get the job done alone. The Israelites repeatedly disobeyed God's commands. They lusted for the possessions of the Canaanites (Achan's Gold), they elected to fight without God's direction (failure at Ai) and they sought peace with the enemies of God (Joshua signed a treaty with the Gibeonites). [Note: This is Israel's first such covenant with the world and we now await Israel's last covenant with the world!] Joshua grew very old and tired of war and **the scepter** was passed to the last Hebrew, his friend Caleb. Now Joshua was of the tribe of Ephraim and, therefore, of the House of Joseph, and Caleb was of the House of Judah.

It is through this symbolic linkage that the scepter of Israel goes over to the House of Judah through which Jesus will come [Caleb is the great-great uncle of Salmon, the great-great grandfather of David] (1 Chronicles 2:9-11). This symbolic transfer of authority is confirmed by God in Judges 1:1-2. After the death of Joshua, God is asked, "Who will be the first (to fight)?"

"The Lord answered, 'Judah' is to go, I have given the land into their hands." But Judah does not get the job done and the other tribes fair equally as bad.

The land remains filled with "Canaanites" (sinners). This sad situation continues until a 'man after God's own heart' leads Israel.

The symbolic fulfillment of the cleansing of the land is finally accomplished at the **end** of the 480 year period by David, a man of war. David fights valiantly for the Lord and finally succeeds in putting "all His enemies under his feet." This takes David's whole life. In his zeal, David also wanted to build the Temple for the Lord but was not allowed. It was David's son, Solomon, a man of peace (rest) who finally built the Temple.

David and Solomon represent two types of Jesus - David is the conquering king who cleanses the land <u>before</u> the rule of peace by Solomon the "teacher". Both of these 'reigns' are direct prophecy of Jesus at the second coming when the land will be cleansed by tribulation and then granted peace in the millennium.

This process of "cleansing the land" for the Kingdom of God is highly prophetic. The first effort to cleanse the land (by Joshua) represents Jesus' first advent. We see in Joshua (of the house of Joseph) the "Jesus, son of Joseph" having His efforts and goals rejected by Israel. Then we see the work completed by the warrior/shepherd, the "Jesus Son of David". Then there is peace. This sequence is a clear picture of Jesus (son of Joseph the carpenter) and His Kingdom being rejected by Israel **until** Jesus, Son of God, the warrior of tribulations, finally cleanses the land. Then there is peace for 1,000 years. This is the classic two Messiah picture.

It is worth mentioning here that some of the post-exilic rabbis taught two (2) Messiah's, one now and one later. The first Messiah was Bar Joseph (son of Joseph) and the second was Bar David.

A. Edersheim and J. Good both expound on this dual Messiah concept, but Good adds the keen understanding that this dual "Messiahship" was what John the Baptist was referring to when he inquired of Jesus, "Are you the one or should we look for another?" (Matthew 11:3) John was not confused or losing faith in the Jesus he baptized. He saw the Holy Spirit land on Jesus. He knew Jesus was **a** Messiah. John simply wondered if Jesus was **both** the first Messiah, Bar Joseph, and the second Messiah, Bar David. (two Messiah's in one!)

John's question is therefore:... "should Israel (the nation) look for a second (different) Messiah after the sacrifice of the Lamb." Jesus' answer was <u>clear</u> to John—Yes, He (Jesus) was <u>both</u> Messiah's and yes, He would <u>come again</u>!

Therefore, let's take a closer look at what clues we can find that point to this second coming.

The graphic of the big picture must now include the war/peace interface of David and Solomon, as well as the Joshua initiated cleansing process. (See Figure 12-3 for the next level of complexity)

We can now identify the physical player(s) in the Sin of Israel. While it is clear that the spiritual component was a failure to trust in, believe in, rest in God -

the physical component was a "disturbance" to the salvation time-line. [Note: This implies that sin (rebellion) changes (delays) "time"! (Salvation/redemption) Think about it. For God is *"long-suffering, to usward, not willing that any should perish* (2 Peter 3:9bKJV)] Joshua divides the land by lot after six years of war. [Notice the imperfect 6 years here, vice a perfect 7 years in the tribulation.] Joshua dies leaving Judah in charge. The delay (in the cleansing process) caused initially by Judah was then adopted by the rest of the tribes in their failure to conquer the inhabitants of the "land." It is now 1400 BC, but the war is not prosecuted in the heart (spiritually) again until David is King in 1010 BC — a delay of 390 years. This delay is the Sin of Israel that God enumerates in Ezekiel 4. To this original stubbornness (of 390 years) the Lord adds 40 years for Judah's leadership failure, giving the nation a total sin penalty of 430 years. Now all three historic periods can be seen to signify 430 years of sin: 430 years of slavery in paganism, 430 years wasted living with pagans (accepting sin) in the land, and 430 years of the Temple cult in pagan Hypocrisy. See Figure 12-3.

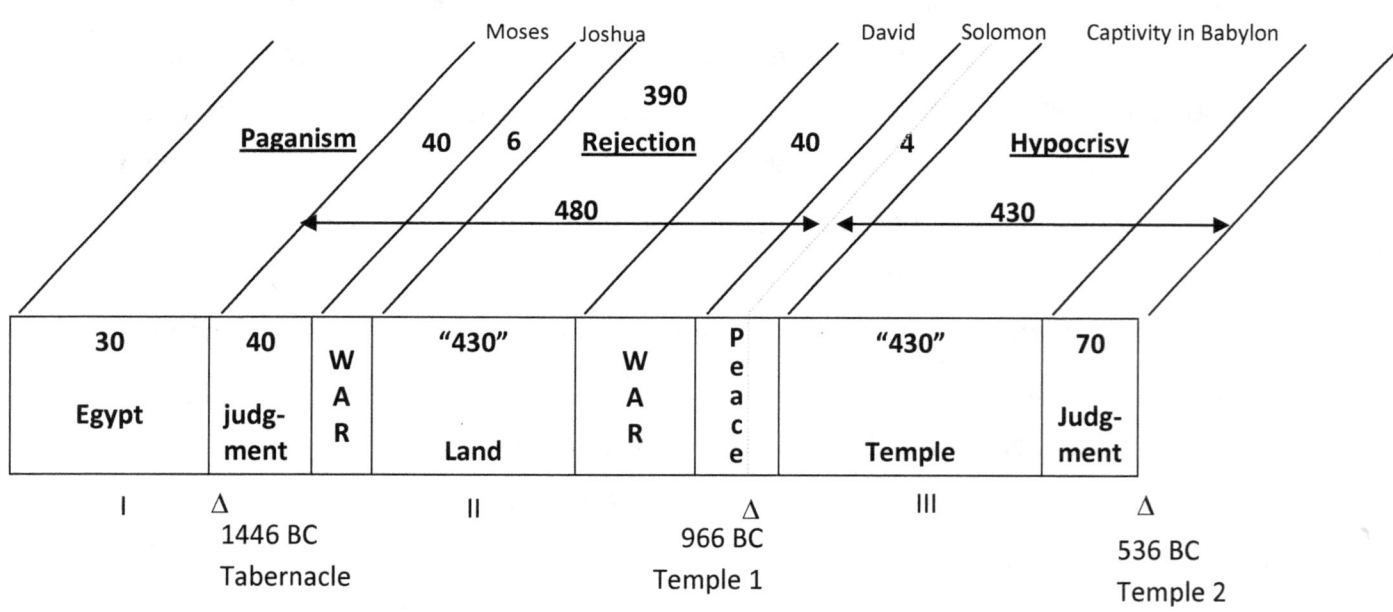

Figure 12-3
430 x 3

[Note also that for Block II, the "430" sin years in the land becomes 480 again by adding 50 years — the time of one Jubilee - when the land is RESTORED, when all things are made new. This theme of "the missed Jubilee" will repeat several times until it is finally achieved in Christ during the millennium.]

We know that God's covenants, His promises to Abraham, Moses, the people, David, etc., always involve the same three major components of **seed**, **land** and **blessing**. Seed (Messiah), Land (Kingdom), and Blessing (Rest) are, in a way, one and the same or a trinity. When offered the **land** initially (after the Exodus), the Jews rejected the <u>land</u>, therefore they also rejected the <u>rest</u>, and wandered 40 years till all the unfaithful were dead (they shall not enter my rest) (Psalm 95:11).

Finally, under Joshua, the people entered the **land** (a clear foreshadowing of the saved entering the Kingdom under the rule of King Jesus, the Messiah.)

So why a penalty of 430 years? Why was the sin of the House of Israel 390 years and the sin of the House of Judah 40 years? Did our Holy and righteous God just pick these numbers at random? Of course not!

The answer lies with "who" entered the **land** and "who" rejected the **blessing (rest)**. We know from Scripture that 12 tribes left Egypt, but not all 12 tribes entered the **land**. Gad, Ruben and half of Manasseh remained on the east side of the Jordan. Does this mean nine-and-one-half tribes entered the **land** (12 - 2.5 = 9.5)? No!! Joshua calls Manasseh a "tribe" because Manasseh and Ephraim were so large. The term is one of convenience and not legality. Note that in Numbers 26, when the second census was taken tribe by tribe, that Ephraim and Manasseh are counted together as the House of Joseph. (In the first census, they are also counted together—see Numbers 1:32.) And in Ezekiel 48 of the twelve gates in the Holy City, one is named Joseph and in Ezekiel 47, Joseph is to receive a double inheritance (not Manasseh and Ephraim individually). This is important because while Joshua gave both Manasseh and Ephraim a separate tribal inheritance (piece of the **land**) because of their size, the Scriptural record of deed holders continues to treat the descendants of Joseph as one tribe.

Therefore, those tribes who remained east of the Jordan were Gad (one tribe), Ruben (one tribe), and half the descendants of Manasseh (one half of Manasseh equals one quarter of the house of Joseph). Thus 9.75 tribes entered the **land**.

Why is this important? Because God gave to each tribe who claimed an inheritance in the **land** the same penalty for rejecting His **rest** (…cleansing of the land = cleansing of the heart…) that He gave to the nation collectively when they rejected the **land** in Numbers 14. Forty years to each heir. This would be then a penalty of 40 years to Judah, Benjamin, Simeon, Zebulun, Issachar, Asher, Naphtali, and Dan (40 times 8 equals 320). To Levi, 40 more years making 360 years (Note: Levi did not receive **land** as inheritance since God was their great reward. But Levi died in the desert for refusing the **blessing** (**rest**) and the same is true here as well.) (Also, see Ezekiel 8-15 and note especially the unfaithfulness of the elders and priesthood in Ezekiel 8:12-18). And lastly to Joseph, now only 3/4 of the tribe, 30 years. (¾ x 40 = 30) Therefore the total for House of Israel is 390 years! When Judah failed to make war on "evil" and chose to live with evil rather than fight, the rest of the nation followed them into defeat. The prize was theirs for the taking, but they chose physical rest (along side of sin) rather than spiritual war. The reader should note Isaiah 28:12 as God speaks to the northern tribes to whom He said: *"This is the **resting** place, let the weary **rest**" and "This is the place of repose, but they would not listen."*

Note also Isaiah 30:15 "This is what the Sovereign Lord, the Holy One of Israel says: "In repentance and **rest** is your salvation, in quietness and trust is your strength, but you would have none of it."

Thus we understand the 390 years for the House of Israel [all the people (not just the Northern tribes), the way Ezekiel used the term]. But for the House of Judah, an additional 40 years! Why? Please note Isaiah 40:2 where God says to Jerusalem, "That she has received from the hand of the Lord double for all her sins." So for the tribe of Judah, we have 40 years included in the 390 for failure to **rest** and then to the House of Judah an additional 40 years to double the penalty (390 + 40 = 430). After all it was Judah's responsibility to cleanse the land and they failed miserably.

In the 430 years penalty we recall the words of Exodus 12:40, *"Now the sojourning of the children of Israel, who dwelt in Egypt, was four hundred and thirty years."* (KJV) That this number (430) should appear twice in Jewish history is surely not by accident. The Sin penalty of 430 years surely speaks loudly of a time in slavery, not physically in Egypt, but Spiritually in Egyptian bondage to sin. Why else would the anointing of the Messiah include the provision to "proclaim freedom for the captives and release for the prisoners" (Isaiah 61:1) . (Please dear God, teach us how to **rest**, how to be free of Egypt, free of bondage, free of sin and free of worry, because those whom the Son sets free are free indeed.)

13.0 THE BIG PICTURE
AS PROPHECY

There is now one more step in seeing the Big Picture — the last step — the prophetic nature of this picture.

The battle that Joshua began and David symbolized - the battle to cleanse the land - will be completed in Daniel's 70th week. The peace and rest that is pictured in David's lesser son, Solomon, will be made perfect in David's greater son, Jesus. This is clearly pictured in the graphic, but how is it prophesied?

We saw that the number of days to Messiah was correctly found by expanding the 69 weeks of Daniel to 173,880 days using Anderson's conversion of 360/365.25 Holy days per regular earth year.

Then we saw that when this conversion factor was tested on other prophecy, it also gave **precise** results.

1. The Babylonian Captivity = 69 solar years
2. The Time of Israel's rebirth = 1948
3. The date of Government = 25 January 1949

Can we apply Anderson to this picture and gain any greater understanding? Yes!

We will look at two cases: one that involves Anderson's conversion and Jeffrey's application of the "seven times" rule according to Leviticus 26. Then we will look at a case just involving the "seven times" rule without the Anderson conversions.

The 'seven times' rule is found in Leviticus 26:18 (and in Leviticus 26:27) where God says to Israel about her punishment for disobedience: "If after all this you will not listen to me, I will punish you for your sins seven times over".

SPECIAL NOTE:

In the following sections, the author will attempt to show, with Scriptural support, independent approaches to determining the month and year of the Lord's return. There have been many attempts to predict the return of Jesus and all have met with failure and embarrassment. The author does not consider himself a prophet. The following insights are gleaned from Scripture and are humbly and respectfully submitted to the church (the body of Christ) for prayerful consideration and with a fervent hope that God may be glorified, Amen.

There are several subjects that must be addressed to adequately cover the fulfillment of an end times projection. These include, but are not limited to:

- The completion of the times of the Gentiles
- The placement of the tribulation
- The return of the Glory of the Lord
- The second advent of Jesus Christ

The following sections present this time line. The reader is requested to recall three insights into the end times.

1. From Daniel 12, we know that end-time knowledge will increase. Not just the explosion of secular and academic knowledge that we have all lived through in the twentieth century, but an increase of Bible knowledge and wisdom as well. Both have been amazing.

2. Joel promises an increase in the Holy Spirit and an increase in dreams and visions. This too is upon us. (Praise God!)

3. Jesus says, "*No one knows the day or the hour*" of His return (<u>as a husband to claim His Bride</u>), but we are told to watch and pray and know the signs of the times. We are not to be caught unaware. Therefore it is possible that we might be given insight as to the year and perhaps the season or even the month of Jesus' return (<u>as Commander of the Army of God and King of Israel</u>.) Oh, yes! Thank you, Father!

It is because God is the same yesterday, today and forever that we may put all our trust in Him. His prophecies of the past were fulfilled precisely, so one is justified in assuming that prophecies of the future will be similarly fulfilled precisely. Pray that we rightly divide the Word.

And nothing is in Scripture without purpose. "My Word... will not return to Me void" (Isaiah 55:11)(KJV). The most insignificant detail has purpose in God's Word. The Spirit may not reveal that purpose until the fullness of time, so increased knowledge and mystery are revealed as necessary to accomplish His purpose. May this be so now.

[Note: there are three types of "years" in this work:
1. Solar years of 365.25 days; and,
2. Biblical lunar years of 354 days; and,
3. Prophetic Holy years of 360 days.]

Lengthy periods (such as 10 or more years) measured in Biblical lunar years can be treated the same as solar years in mathematical operations. This is because the Biblical lunar year is adjusted to track with the solar year by the insertion of a 13th month (2nd Adar) every other year of so. An accuracy of ± 20 days or so can be expected. (E.g. 40 Biblical lunar years will be within one lunar cycle of 40 solar years).

The term 'years' can apply to either solar or lunar years unless it is specified in the text for purposes of calendar consistency or seasonal tracking (i.e. finding New Year's Day or Pentecost, etc.)

'Prophetic Holy Years' is another story altogether. These years are always 360 days each and there are no adjustments. The Prophetic clock slews off from the solar clock quickly - at a rate of +5.25 days per solar year. For a quick rule of thumb, 70 Prophetic Holy Years is 69 solar years (within 2 days).

All Bible prophecy, whether verbal or historical allegory, is given in Prophetic Holy years. All Biblical events are measured in Biblical lunar years (except Noah's Flood which provides the standard for measuring Prophetic Holy years!).

Case 1: Prophecy on Cleansing

Israel was ordered to cleanse the land, but they failed to obey God. The cleansing wars of Joshua and David are symbolic of the cleansing that God Himself will accomplish in the land. The last cleansing war is the Tribulation where Christ's enemies are placed into subjugation and Israel is prepared to receive her King. Without the adverse impacts of sin, Moses would have led the people into the Promised Land (the Kingdom) in 1445 BC, but that was not to be the case. The people balked in the desert, and this caused 'delay' (38.6 years). Joshua and Judah failed in cleansing the land and this bought more delay (390 years). Thus the symbolic cleansing 'War' was protracted all the way to David's reign. When will the final (actual) tribulation/cleansing process occur?

We will use the 480-year block as an Ebenezer, a "memorial stone", to prophesy and project the answer. The entire 480 years block of time is, in essence, a "Prophecy Block".

The 480-year period represents "history" from Exodus to Tribulation (final cleansing), but certain years do not apply. The sin period wandering the desert is a separate piece of time inserted into history for a single purpose — the symbolic death penalty for those who refused to enter the land. These 38.6 years <u>do not apply here</u>. The 480-year block also includes 4 years of Solomon's reign, which, as pre-millennium administration, <u>do not apply here</u>. (This will be explained in greater detail in Chapter 15.) Since the original process of cleansing the land was not completed, we will multiply the remaining sin period by the Leviticus 26 admonition adjusted with the Anderson coefficient as follows:

```
    480    years of prophecy
  -38.6    desert penalty (which does not apply)
   -4.0    Solomon's reign (which does not apply)
  437.4    years of cleansing failure
     x7    according to Leviticus 26
 3,061.8   Prophetic Holy years
    x[A]   Anderson's Coef. 360/365.25
 3,017.8   Biblical years to the cleansing of the land — the
           Tribulation
```

We see that this process projects the final cleansing of the land to be over three thousand years into the future — three thousand years from <u>what</u>? Three thousand years from the <u>symbolic</u> enactment of this event pictured in the Prophecy Block — <u>David's symbolic cleansing</u>. David (as a type of Jesus) begins the cleansing process when he becomes King of Judah in 1010 BC. <u>Therefore</u>,

```
  3017.8   years to Tribulation
 -1010.X   start of symbolic tribulation
```
problem!

[Note: Sound mathematics requires that the years before Christ (BC) be expressed as decimals representing "length of time" to the zero point (<u>not zero year</u>). Thus halfway through 1010 BC (June/July of 1010 BC) in the Julian calendar would be written as 1009.5. Since the Prophetic Block is based on the Biblical lunar calendar, the year begins and ends two weeks before Passover — about mid April. David ruled Judah seven and a half years. Therefore, David's rise to the throne of Judah is probably a fall of 1010 BC event and best approximated as 1009.7 BC]

Using the time expression standard given above we now find the prophecy calculation to compute as follows:

```
 3,017.8    Years to Tribulation
-1,009.3    Start of Symbolic Tribulation
 2,008.5    Start of actual Tribulation
```

This is approximately 1 ¼ months into the year 2009 — based on the Hebrew Religious new year — or sometime in the month of Tishri in the Fall of 2009 AD. [See Appendix I Error Analysis for the accuracy of the dates.]

****

Special note: The dating of Solomon's reign (and therefore David's reign) and the building of the temple can be accomplished with reasonable precision. The following excerpt is taken from the Zondervan NIV Study Bible Introduction to 1 Kings Chronology Section, Paragraph 2:

> "By integrating Biblical data with those derived from Assyrian chronological records, the year 853 BC can be fixed as the year of Ahab's death, and the year 841 as the year Jehu began to reign. The years in which Ahab and Jehu had contacts with Shalmaneser III of Assyria can also be given definite dates (by means of astronomical calculations based on an Assyrian reference to a solar eclipse). With these fixed points, it is then possible to work both forward and backward in the lines of the kings of Israel and Judah to

give dates for each king. By the same means it can be determined that the division of the kingdom occurred in 930, that Samaria fell to the Assyrians in 722-721 and that Jerusalem fell to the Babylonians in 586."

Additional support is found in Edwin E. Thiele's book <u>The Mysterious Numbers of the Hebrew Kings</u> (Eerdman's Publishing, Grand Rapids, Michigan.) Interested readers are directed to Chapter 3: "The Establishment of an Absolute Date in Hebrew Chronology".

Knowing that the kingdom was divided in 930 BC and that Solomon reigned 40 years (I Kings 11:42), places his ascension to the throne in 970 BC.

When Solomon came to the throne can be further narrowed down by noting that 1 Kings 6:1 and 6:38 reads:

> *"In the fourth year of Solomon's reign over Israel,*
> *in the month of Ziv, the second month, he began*
> *to build the temple of the Lord."*

and

> *"In the eleventh year in the month of Bul, the eighth*
> *month, the temple was finished in all its details*
> *according to its specifications."*

If Ziv 966 BC is in Solomon's 4th year and if Bul of 959 BC is in Solomon's 11th year, he had to take the throne sometime late in 970.....sometime after the 8th month (otherwise Bul of 959 BC would be in his 12th year), but before Tebeth, the 10th month - otherwise his 40 year reign would have extended past 930 BC on the Julian calendar when the kingdom was divided (after his death).

Additionally 2 Samuel 5:4 tells us David reigned 40 years and verse 5 says:

> *"In Hebron he reigned over Judah seven years and six months, and*
> *in Jerusalem he reigned over all Israel and Judah 33 years.."*

This gives us an obvious problem. 7 ½ years plus 33 years equals 40 ½ years. But the previous verse said David ruled 40 years. Why would accuracy to the month in verse 5 contradict the message in verse 4? <u>Well it doesn't!!</u> Look at the following figure.

110

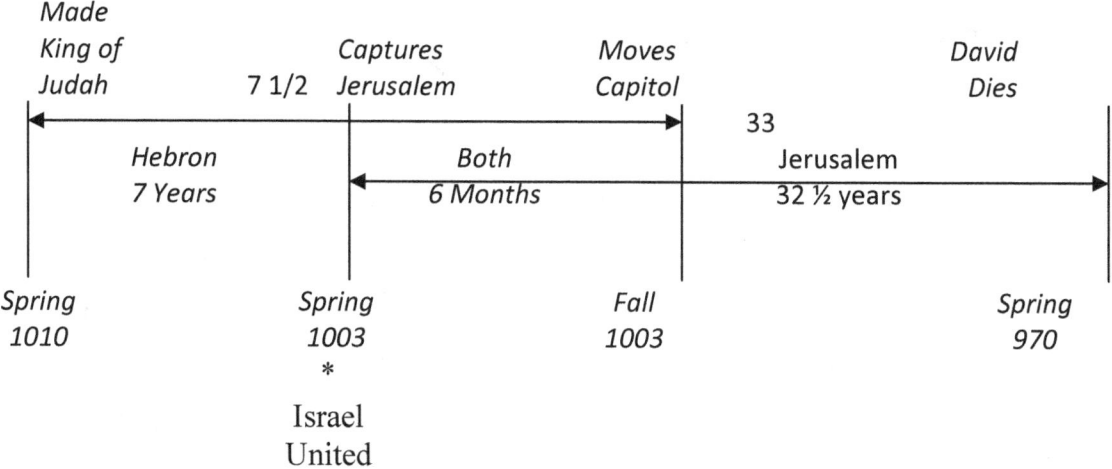

David's Combined Reign

David reigned seven years over Judah in Hebron. Seven years before uniting Israel under one king and capturing Judah. [This is a powerful prophetic image of the tribulation!!] Although the government of 1000BC was not as cumbersome as today's, it still took time to move the capitol from Hebron to Jerusalem. The populous of Hebron had to be pacified. Defenses had to be established and all of the offices of bureaucracy had to be relocated, and their families and belongings, etc. It took six months to effect the relocation! Thus the six month "discrepancy" is really a History lesson that reinforces the perfection of Scripture. We have two points of regency during the transitions of Government. David did reign for 40 years. The 7 ½ years and the 33 years overlap for six months.

If Solomon succeeds in late 970 BC (Probably Kislev, the 9th month) then 40 years earlier puts David's ascension in the fall of 1010 BC or about −1009.3 algebraically.

Thus we have for the dating of Solomon's reign (and David's reign) an accuracy of ± one month or about .1 years.

Perhaps there are even finer methodologies available for the reconstruction of the prophetic chronologies, but an accuracy of .1 years is adequate for this work.

****

The second example of prophecy coming out of this big picture is the arrival and departure of the Glory of the Lord. We have seen that the prophecy/history Ebenezer (the 480 year period) ends with the exile and the captivity in Babylon, the 70 years of Jeremiah so the land could have its Sabbath rest.

We have seen that the period between the Temples (430 years) is tied to the Jew's failure (and our failure) to **rest** (trusting completely in God). It is because Jesus so trusted God that He can give us **rest** now. "*Come unto me... and I will give you rest*" (Matthew 11:28)(KJV)!

Let's look at the foundation of the first Temple. Why did God make David wait to build the Temple? Because David was a man of war, not **rest**. Solomon, who was a man of **rest** and peace (See I Samuel 22:9, 10), would build the Temple where God's name would **rest**. (This clearly foreshadows Jesus building the true Temple.) But there is more. Note that I Kings 6:1 says:

> "*In the 480th year after the Israelites had come out of Egypt, in the fourth year of Solomon's reign over Israel, in <u>the month of Ziv</u>, the second month, he began to build the Temple of the Lord.*"

Solomon succeeded to the throne just prior to David's death in 970 BC. The fourth year of Solomon's reign would be 966 BC. If we go back 480 years, we are in the year 1446 BC.

The first Passover and the exodus were in the first month, the month of Nisan and the giving of the 10 commandments was at Pentecost in the third month (Sivan). So, if we go back precisely 480 years from the first Temple foundation, we land between the Passover and Pentecost. But, do we find anything significant between the Passover and the Pentecost in the month of Ziv (the second month)? Oh yes, <u>the very first Sabbath</u>, the <u>very first day of</u> **rest**.

In Exodus 16, we find the Jews in the desert grumbling because they were out of food. This in on the 15th of Ziv. And that evening "**the Glory of the Lord** appeared in a cloud" for the first time to the children of Israel. And the Lord sent them quail at twilight and bread (manna) in the morning. And the manna was gathered for 6 days. Then in verse 23, the Lord declares the 7th day to be Holy, a Sabbath, a day of **rest**. (Previously In Exodus 16:4, God tells Moses that this is a <u>test</u> to see if the people will obey.) So the 21st of Ziv becomes the very first Sabbath. Our first day of **rest**, was given to us even before the Law, which was given two weeks later. Did the Jews pass the test? Exodus 16:27 says, "*Nevertheless, some of the people went out on the seventh day to gather it (manna) but they found none*"!! They failed the test. They failed to **rest**.

So while "Israel ate manna forty years" (Exodus 16:34), they failed to **rest**.

And it was 12 tribes times 40 years or 480 years to the month (maybe to the day?) before God allowed the Temple to be built and **the test** of Sabbath **rest** to resume.

So of all of Israel's sins, idolatry, adultery, murder and abominations of all unrighteousness, God chose to prosecute, convict, and incarcerate His people for their worst sin. But not just any sin, that sin which is at the heart of the covenant (both old and new) to **rest**, to **rest** in God, to **rest** in promise, to **rest** in belief, to **rest** in faith (and faith is an action verb not a state of mind). The missing action was **rest**!. How like our God to give us such a mystery. We must act by **resting**. Praise God.

The significance of the appearance of the Glory of the Lord to the children of Israel cannot be understated. God had chosen this people to make His name known. It was this Glory that would lead His chosen through the wilderness, that would dwell among them in the tabernacle (tent of meeting). It was this Glory that would fill the Temple and it was this Glory that would **rest** on the nation of Israel. If they would only obey and let God be what He is, sovereign, and **rest** in and with Him.

The presence of the Glory of the Lord with Israel was a partial fulfillment of the covenant promise to Abraham in Genesis 15:1 "... *I am thy shield and thy exceeding great reward.*" (KJV) But there was a price to pay for this reward, even in partial fulfillment. Israel would serve God's purpose in making His name great by being put in slavery in Egypt 430 years.

(Note: There is some debate whether this period of servitude begins when the promise is actually given to Abraham or when Jacob descends into Egypt. The issue is over the counting of "four generations". But this chronology dispute is beyond the scope of this work.)

So God used Israel as His tool or instrument in executing His perfect plan of redemption. Israel suffered terribly during this period of servitude. But, God in His perfect righteousness, would reward them <u>double</u> for their trouble. You will recall that some years earlier God had used Job in similar servitude to glorify His name. Although Job lost everything (but his faith) God restored to him <u>double</u> for his service (everything but the original children who were not Job's to begin with, but God's). The reader should also note that in Deuteronomy 21, the first born son is to receive a <u>double</u> portion of inheritance and also in Deuteronomy 15, a slave is worth <u>double</u> that of a hired servant.

Therefore God, who is true, allowed His Glory to dwell among the children of Israel for 860 years (430 x 2). (Recall God's words to Abraham: "*I Am...your exceedingly great reward*". Genesis 15:1 (KJV)) This 860 year period is measured from His first appearance in the wilderness in 1446 BC to the destruction of Jerusalem by Nebuchadnezzer in 586 BC for a total of 860 years. Although other Temples were built by Zerubabbal and Herod, this reward, God's Glory, <u>did not</u> return to Israel.

It is this choice of God's Glory not to return to Israel following the return from captivity that clearly shows the nation to still be under judgment (as noted earlier [see Chapter 9]. In his book <u>Armageddon</u> Jeffrey subtracts the 70 years of captivity (time actually served) from the original 430-year sentence and multiplies the remaining 360 years (of Israel's probation) by 7 [A]. This product is then added to the year 536 BC wherein Jeffrey discovered that Israel's banishment would last until 1948 AD. I believe the choice of the Glory of the Lord **not** to reappear in Israel or in the Temple confirms Jeffrey's assumption.).But the Glory of the Lord **does** return to Israel. This event is described in Ezekiel 43 and following. The Glory of the Lord returns to the millennial Temple!

So God was faithful to Israel, remaining with them from the wilderness to captivity. Once the captivity was over, Israel was again returned to the **land**, but on probation. Yet Israel still refused to repent and accept the full measure of the trinity covenant: **seed** (Messiah and righteousness), **land** (kingdom), and **blessing** (**rest**, relationship, and surrender to God's rule - your exceeding great reward!)

Therefore, God applied the sevens times penalty (of Leviticus 26). Yet during the dispensation of Law, God also offered grace through Jesus the Christ (*Come to me all ye who labor and are heavy laden and I will give you **rest***) and yet again it was rejected, resulting in the destruction of the Temple and the world wide Diaspora.

At this point, the table of covenant violations looks like this:

VIOLATION	WHEN/WHERE	OFFENDER	PENALTY
Rejection of Sabbath- **Rest**	1446 BC in the desert (Pre-law)	All twelve tribes	40 years per tribe without Temple
Rejection of the **land**	1445 BC in the desert (Post-law)	All twelve tribes	Death, 40 years of wandering for survivors
Rejection of Sabbath rest for the **land**	966-536 BC in the land	9 ¾ tribes, the heirs	430 years = 70 served in captivity, 360 on probation x 7[A] = 2483 actual years. Nationhood returned in 1948
Rejection of seed (**Messiah**)	32 AD in the **land**	All Israel	Destruction of Jerusalem, 70 AD - Global Diaspora

TABLE 13-1
COVENANT VIOLATIONS

Since the seed is the Messiah of the kingdom all three, **seed**, **rest**, and **land,** are withheld from Israel in 32 AD.

Today (post 1948) Israel is back in the **land** and the eternal covenant of **seed, land, rest** is still being offered and ignored. This time God will punish Israel as **never before**. The tribulation, "The time of Jacob's trouble", is at hand

... but when?

How long will God endure Israel's rejection of His **rest** this time before He acts?

[Note: Romans 11:26 tells us: *"and so all Israel will be saved...."* Therefore God's wrath toward Israel will be satisfied and His perfect love and mercy will again be manifest toward His chosen people. This event is predicted by the timetable of the Noahic flood. The salvation of 'all Israel' occurs during the fourth manifestation of **the 3rd day of the Glory of the Lord.** This salvation will occur with the fulfillment of the prophecy of Zechariah 12:10: *"...and they shall look upon me whom they have pierced, and they shall mourn..."* (KJV) This mourning is the repentance of Israel. God will lift the veil from off their eyes and they will accept Jesus as King/Messiah. This subject is discussed at length in Chapter 17.]

We note that Scripture (which is given by the Holy Spirit) often makes reference to God's precision such as in Exodus 12:41 when the Word states "to the very day". Anderson's work in rightly dividing the Word of Daniel 9:24,25 similarly produces fulfillment that is "to the very day". Isaiah repeatedly states that God's time-independent omniscience is what marks Him as the "One and Only". The author will now make an assumption based on this precept and that is:

ASSUMPTION

That the Glory of the Lord departed from Israel precisely after 860 years, "to the very day". This was Israel's double **blessing** and this is why the day and date of the first appearance of the Glory of the Lord is given in Exodus 16.

Case 2: Return of the Glory of the Lord

In Ezekiel 10, we read that the Glory of the Lord departed from the Temple. A day and date is not given, but we know the general time frame. The vision begins in Ezekiel 8:1 "In the sixth year, in the sixth month on the fifth day."

This is in reference to the exile of King Jehoiachin (see Ezekiel 1:2). So this vision can be dated to September of 592 BC. The questions is: Is this vision seen while the events were occurring or does it depict future events? Since the total vision (Ezekiel 8-11) includes the destruction of Jerusalem (and Israel's leaders) and since the succeeding chapters of Ezekiel also deal with future events, it is assumed that the vision of Ezekiel 10 also represents events still in the future. Therefore, since the Glory of the Lord first came to Israel on 15 Ziv 1446 BC, we will assume an 860 year presence (measured in Jewish lunar years according to the Biblical calendar in figure 2-1) until 15 Ziv 586 BC, three months before the final destruction of Jerusalem and the Temple (7 Ab 586 BC).

We will now test this assumption and examine the consequences. We know from Ezekiel 43 that the Glory of the Lord will return to the millennial Temple. But when did the Glory of the Lord enter Solomon's Temple and how long did He reside there? From I Kings 6:37,38, we know that Solomon began building the Temple in the 4th year, in the month of Ziv, 966 BC and completed the construction "in the 11th year in the month of Bul, the eighth month"; that would be in 959 BC. It took 7 years to build the Temple. The Temple furnishings were then installed (I Kings 7:13 ff) and preparations were made to bring the Ark of the Covenant into the Temple during the Feast of Tabernacles (I Kings 8:2) in the seventh month of Ethanim (later renamed Tishri) in 958 BC. We know from Leviticus 23 that the Feast of Tabernacles lasts from the 15th –21st of Tishri. It begins with a sacred assembly and ends with another sacred assembly on the 22nd of Tishri,

It is reasonable to believe that the events of I Kings 8 (the placing of the ark in the Holy of Holies and Solomon's prayer of dedication) occurred during one of the two sacred assemblies. Did Solomon begin the Feast by dedicating the Temple or save this for the grand finale? We will assume and try the former.

Note from I Kings 8:11 that *"The Glory of the Lord filled His Temple."* Thus the Glory of the Lord remained in the Temple from 15 Tishri 958 BC until the completion of the 860 years, that is until 15 Ziv 586 BC. The length of time (in Biblical lunar years) that the Glory resided in the Temple can be computed as follows:

- A) The 15th of Tishri is 162 days from the end of the Biblical lunar year (a year of 354 days). This gives us a residual of .46 years.
- B) The 15th of Ziv is 45 days into the Biblical lunar year or a residual of .13 years.
- C) Thus from 957 BC to 587 BC is 371 years (inclusive) plus the residuals (.46 +.13) giving us a total of 371.6 Biblical lunar years.

As noted earlier, Grant Jeffrey subtracted the 70 years served by Israel from her total sentence of 430 years and considered the 360 year remainder as probation. This remainder he multiplied by 7[A] (See Leviticus 26:18) to determine when the Jews would return to the land (1948).

Because the Glory of the Lord did not return to Israel with their return from captivity but has remained <u>absent to this day</u>, we will apply the Levitical multipliers of 7 to the 371.6 years. This yields 2601.2 years of absence. From 15 Ziv 586 BC (which is –585.8 lunar) (when the Glory departed) we go forward 2601.2 years, which gives us 2015.4 (lunar) or sometime in 2016 AD.

Since Tishri of 2016 would begin on 2015.5, our date of 2015.4 is .1 years before the Feast of Trumpets in 2016 AD. This is about the 1st of Elul 2016. In Chapter 15 we will show by a different prophecy that the sign of the Son of Man will begin on the 1st of Elul. Since the appearance of this sign marks the beginning of the return of Jesus it is also the beginning of the return of the Glory of the Lord. (Praise God!)

[Note: The Anderson coefficient [A] does not apply here. The Glory rested 371.6 **_real_** years and the absence is seven times this number. The answer is in real years - no prophecy is involved.]

The examples shown in this section are only two cases taken from the "Big Picture." Several more examples of fulfilled prophecy and future predictions will be examined in the following sections. The correlation of the Tribulation to David's Wars seems valid and the Arrival and Departure of the Glory of the Lord is straightforward.

Let's look at two other cases of prophecy from <u>other</u> time periods. Case 3 will be Hosea's prophecy concerning the times of the Gentiles (Hosea 6.2) and

Case 4 will be the advent of Zion's (Israel's) first Jubilee.

Case 3: THE TIMES OF THE GENTILES

Most Bible students would agree that the term "the times of the Gentiles" as used by Jesus in Luke 21:24 refers to a sub-mystery of the church, specifically the gift of the Holy Spirit to the Gentile believers. The Holy Spirit was first given to believers (the church) on Pentecost 32 AD (based on Anderson's chronology). From its meager beginning, the church grew quickly to several thousand believers. But these were Jews, born again Jews. The ruling establishment of that day persecuted the church vigorously until sometime after Paul's conversion and his first meeting with Peter (following Paul's seclusion in Damascus/Arabia for three years). It was after this meeting between Peter and Paul that the church had some **rest** (Acts 9:31).

It was during this **rest** that Peter was called to lay hands on Cornelius and the Gentile world received the Holy Spirit. The times of the Gentiles had begun. The NIV chronologies place this event at about 38 AD. There is great significance here. Since the Spirit was given to the Jews first in 32 AD and then to Gentiles in 38 AD, a period of 6 years had elapsed. The gift of the Spirit to the Gentiles happened during the period of **rest**, sometime during the seventh year - the Christian era's first Sabbath year of the Holy Spirit.

Israel has now rejected grace — a concept that includes all three components of the triune covenant: Seed (Messiah), Land (Kingdom), and Blessing (Spirit-Rest).

We know that with the rejection of Jesus and the rejection of the Holy Spirit, Israel suffered the destruction of Jerusalem, the destruction of the Temple and the worldwide scattering of the Jewish people (the Diaspora). Scripture refers to this period in Hosea 6:1-3. Hosea sees God's rejection of Israel lasting but two days, for on the third day He will restore us. While the symbology surely imitates a death and resurrection like Jesus', the reference is primarily to end times and the Word's appearing. Using Peter's insight that with the Lord one day is as a thousand years, we see 2000 prophetic years for the isolation and rejection of Israel. This is the "times of the Gentiles". [Note: Jesus says "times" (plural) not "time" (singular). This same usage appears in Daniel 12:7 and Revelation 12:14. In those cases "times" (plural) means <u>two</u> - specifically two years. Here, we submit, that Jesus means "two days - with the Lord - hence, two thousand years!] Since it will last 2000 prophetic years, we must convert by Anderson's adjustment of 360/365.25, which yields 1971.25 solar (normal) years. If the times of the Gentiles began with Cornelius in 38 AD it will end 1971.25 years later. <u>If</u> Peter's trip to see Cornelius was in the summer of 38 AD (or 37.25 Hebrew/lunar), then adding 1971.25 gives us 2008.5 for the times of the Gentiles to be fulfilled and the <u>return to law</u> and the tribulation to begin. Since the tribulation will last 7 years, we again have the return of the Lord in the 7th month of 2016. (2008.5 + 7 = 2015.5 = fall 2016) This is our third estimate by independent approaches that yields Tishri 2016.

Case 4. The Jubilee Year

The appearance of the Messiah to Israel is a joyous and magnificent celebration. The Scriptures clearly describe it as a time for setting everything right — a time of new beginnings! (*Behold I make all things new.* Revelation 21:5) National restoration is not unfamiliar to the Jew. The Law required debt forgiveness, **land** restoration, slave/prisoner release every 50 years. It was a Jubilee, a year to the Lord. The return of Jesus is **<u>surely</u>** such a year. But Jesus is also known as "The Lord of Glory" (James 2:1). Is it possible that the Jubilee of Messiah is also the same time as the return of the Glory of the Lord?

Israel became a nation in 1948 by a vote of the United Nations. The Jubilee of her nationhood would begin therefore after 49 years have passed or sometime in 1997. However, the Lord's return will be to Jerusalem, with a grand entrance into the Temple. Israel did not acquire the West Bank, Jerusalem, and the Temple mount until the Arab Israel conflict known as the Six Day War of 1967. Israel took the Temple mount during the first week of June 1967. The Jubilee year of this event will begin after 49 years. So to June 1967 we add 49 years and get June 2016 for the Jubilee. But we know from Leviticus 25 that

"Jubilee" begins just prior to sundown on the 10th of Tishri (Leviticus 25:9ff). Therefore, **all 50-year anniversaries**, regardless of when in the calendar year they occur, have their jubilee years all beginning on the same day - sundown on the 10th of Tishri. This was the same month and year estimated for the return of the Glory of the Lord! (See Case 2.)

If these estimates are correct, the tribulation will end sometime in 2016. Since the tribulation, the time of Jacob's trouble is seven years long, the wrath of God will begin sometime in 2009. But the tribulation is normally understood to be the seventieth week of Daniel (see Daniel 9) and this is a period of judgment under the Law, the old Law, covenant Law. This implies that the age of Grace, our present dispensation has ended. But none of this can happen until "the times of the Gentiles be fulfilled." (Tishri 2009 - see Case 3)

In these four cases we arrived at the same answer by four independent methods. And we arrived with the same year and month. This process is shown in figure 13-1. This surely seems like a well-defined process — How can we still say no man knows the day or the hour?

Answer: The time no one knows is for the bride to be ready for the Groom (Rapture) (PTL!!) The Church — the Bride — is not seen in this pictogram Prophecy process. (See Chapter 16) But note how Israel keeps delaying the arrival of Her Messiah by pride and rebellion. First there's hard-heartedness in the failure to trust God to fight the battle (...with the 'giants'). This brings a 40-year penalty then there's another 390 years when it was easier to be mixed with pagans than to be separated. Then 430 years of Temple worship that was cultic in nature and idolatry to God. This third offense drew 2520 years (...a seven times penalty). Thus we have seen the probation of the post-exilic period finally terminate in nationhood... again. So the question becomes 'is Israel preparing for her Savior-King now that they are back in the land (kingdom) again?' He **is** coming!

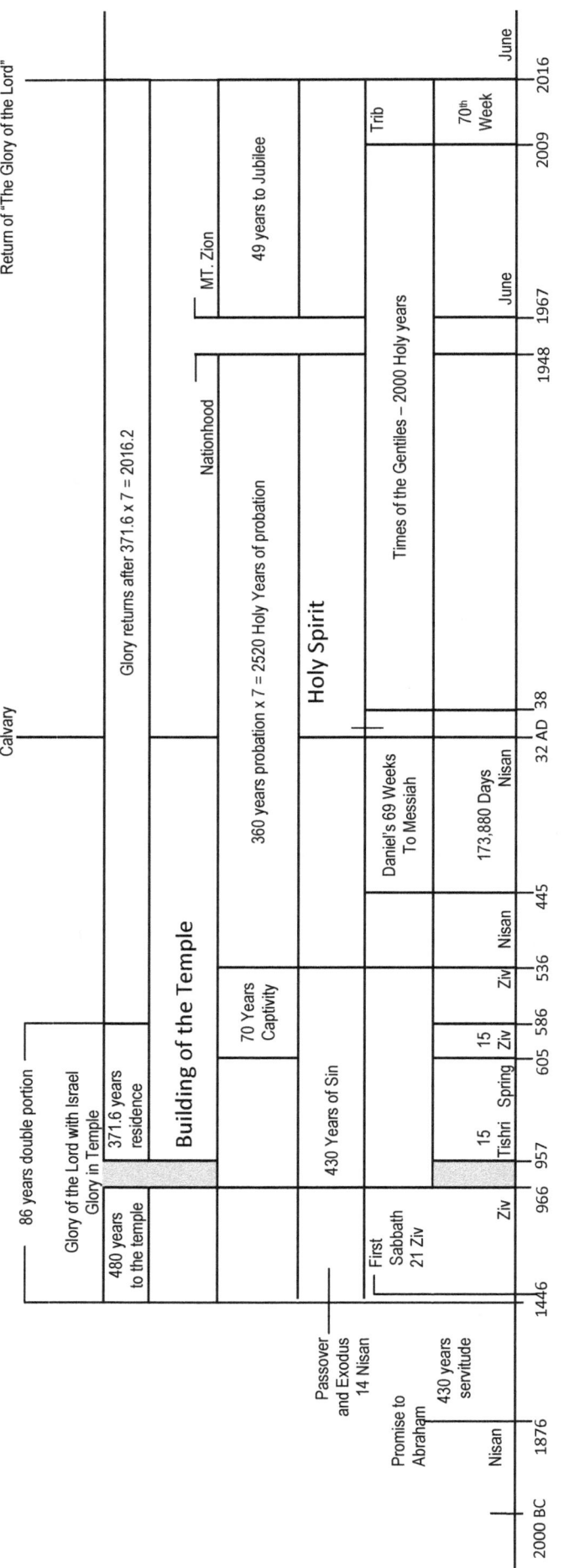

Figure 13-1
GLORY TIMELINE

14.0 Segment Prophecy Block 480

14A A YEAR IS A DAY

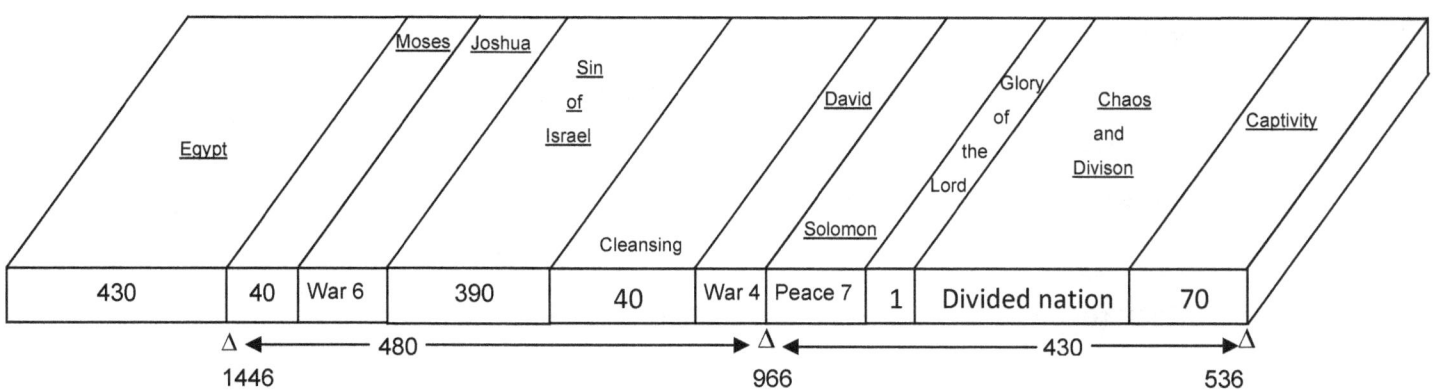

Figure 14A-1
A YEAR IS A DAY - OVERVIEW

As shown in Figure 14A-1, the history of Israel has periods of obedience to God intermixed with periods of rebellion. When we looked at Joshua originally we saw him as a type of Christ — leading his people across the Jordan and leading the army of Israel in the effort to cleanse the land — this was taught as prophecy of the First Messiah, the Messiah Ben (son of) Joseph — the Anointed One from the tribal house of Joseph that would begin Israel's war for independence. The final victory "it was thought" would come through the conquest of the Messiah Ben David.

When we look at Joshua we must ask ourselves (again) what role is Jesus portraying — the answer is found in Joshua 5:13-15. Jesus is now the Commander of the Army of the Lord. It is His job here to do the will of the Father and completely destroy without mercy the enemies of God. Remember, God's command to Joshua was to slaughter without mercy the enemies of God. This is the picture of the Tribulation. This war should have lasted 7 years and was designed to completely cleanse the Promised Land.

If we remove the periods of rebellion from Figure 14A-1 we will see a very different message in the history of Israel. For example, if we remove the 40 years of wandering (Judgment) and the 390 years of Sin for the house of Israel (failure to prosecute the Cleansing War), we can converge the big picture boundaries together until Moses/Joshua joins David/Solomon. In this way we see the Redemption and Cleansing work of God co-joined to the Victory and Peace (rest) components.

The real surprise from this picture comes when we carefully examine the duration of each sub-segment.

Moses leads his people into the Wilderness originally as a function of Worship — **for three days**! Israel followed God through the Red Sea to Mt. Sinai where they received the Law. Israel camped there for almost one year (50 weeks) [3rd Sivan '46 to 20th Ziv '45]. Israel left Sinai and went to inspect the land in the "season of the first Grape Harvest" (Numbers 13). This is sometime in the fourth month (Tammuz). Allowing 40 days (for inspection) should bring us to just about the end of month 5 when Judgment falls — **IF** we call this opening segment 1½ years then we see a picture of Moses and Israel, as a nation, blessed by God for some 1500 years (1½ days).

Recall that God equated a day's sin to a year's penalty in both Genesis and Ezekiel. Therefore, this 1½ years of faithfulness or obedience to God would equate to a day and a half on God's time line. Using Peter's reminder that a day with God is as 1,000 years, then we have a prophecy of 1,500 years of God's blessing in Redemption. Let's convert 1,500 prophetic years to 'real years', and see, if in fact, this segment of history was 'prophecy'.

Prophetic Holy years 1500 x [A] = **1478** Actual years of prophecy.

From the physical redemption of the Exodus   1446 BC
To the spiritual redemption of Messiah Jesus   ± 32 AD
                                            Total   =   **1478** Actual years of redemption history.

Recall that by agreement with Pharaoh Israel was to go <u>out of Egypt</u> for <u>3</u> days in order to Worship. The first Exodus was 1½ years until judgment. The second exodus (from Babylon) was also 1½ years. Together these journeys from sin make 3 days — which of course prefigures the journey of Jesus (more on this in Chapter 16).

14B   DAVID'S YEARS

When we examine the history of the David/Solomon time boundary we get not only a picture of the Tribulation/Millennium Boundary, but also an <u>exact</u> replica of the events of Jesus' return. The projection of history as prophecy provides <u>independent confirmation</u> for our thesis that all history (time) points to Jesus and His return.

Figure 14B-1 represents the Reign of David and the first 12 years of Solomon's reign. In this pictogram we can see the prophetic segments of their respective days. David spent 30 years in war. All of Israel's enemies were put under his feet. Then the land had rest. Then David amassed the material to build the temple. This took David ten years. When Solomon is anointed king, he spends 4 years in administration securing the crown, and then he spends seven years building the Temple and 1 year waiting on the Lord's Glory. This historic pictogram segment is a year/day prophecy. It tells us about the return of Jesus.

30	10	4	7	1
David = 40		Solomon = 12		

Figure 14B-1

A YEAR IS A DAY - COMPRESSION

Jesus is going to return as

    1 - The Warrior Lord

    2 - The Only Son

    3 - The Son of Man

    4 - The High Priest (Judge)

    5 - The King

    6 - The Groom

    7 - The Teacher

        [and others perhaps?]

Jesus tells us that His return is a process that will take a few days. Jesus compares His second coming to the days of Noah and includes the Flood, which swept the unprepared away (so be ready!). This then is the 40 days of Rain or 40 days of Judgment (cleansing). *During this period, Jesus says:*

> *The sun will be darkened,*
>
> *and the moon will not give its light;*
>
> *The stars will fall from the sky,*
>
> *and the heavenly bodies will be shaken. At that*
>
> *time the sign of the Son of Man will appear in the*
>
> *sky, and all the nations of the earth will mourn.*
>
> Matthew 24:29/30

But this picture of the Sign of God in the Heavens already exists in Old Testament Scripture — it is at the Blowing of the Trumpet at the end of the Age. Zechariah 9:14.

> *Then the Lord will appear over them; his arrow will flash*
>
> *like lightning.*
>
> *The Sovereign Lord will sound the Trumpet.*

So all Israel will see this Warrior God. What day are we looking at? The fulfillment of <u>The Feast of Trumpets</u>!! We will also see the fulfillment of Zechariah 12:10ff :

> *They will look on me,*
>
> *The one they have pierced,*
>
> *And they will mourn for him*

> *As one mourns for an only child.*

Ten days later at Yom Kippur the day of Atonement, the veil which has blinded Israel will finally be lifted and Israel will see their Messiah, Jesus.

It is during the ten days from the Feast of Trumpets to the Atonement of Yom Kippur that the Army of Heaven is wiping out all of the enemies of God on the face of the Earth. This will be the most horrible of times. In Hebrew: Yamin Noráim; the days of awe!

Luke 17:34

> *One will be taken*
> *and the other left.*

Matthew 13:30b

> *At that time I will tell the harvesters: First collect the*
> *weeds and tie them in bundles to be burned, then gather*
> *the wheat and bring it into my barn.*

Here "taken" is not taken away in rapture but "taken to be burned" as part of the cleansing process initiated by Joshua 3,500 years earlier. Christ and His warriors will destroy or bind and capture all evil and purge it from the surface of the earth — except for the elect — those humans left to enter into the Millennium with Christ as their present and ruling king.

These are the 10 days Jesus speaks of when addressing His letter to the church at Smyrna — regarding the wrath of Satan:

Revelation. 2:10

> *Do not be afraid of what you are about to suffer...*
> *Persecution for ten days* which is the same message that the
> Scripture provides as encouragement to believers:

Luke 21:18

> *"Not a hair of your head will perish"*

By specifying these 10 days as special or unique, Jesus divided the 40 days of His second coming into two components, one of 30 days and one of 10 days. If we divide David's Reign as King at these same points, 30 years and 10 years, we find a remarkable occurrence at year 30 of his reign (c. 980 BC) and a marked change of emphasis in his activities. Prior to 980 BC David was a man of war committed to the destruction of Israel's enemies. After 980*, David's concerns are with the gathering or "harvesting" of supplies to build the Temple and Solomon's succession to the throne.

[*This is using the chronology provided by the NIV Editors.]

The key event that separated these states of heart was David's Sin of Numbering the Army — taking a census. If the last ten days, the days of awe, correctly corresponds with the angelic harvest — then the census taking privilege belongs to Christ alone (and David understood his error!)

David's sin cost many lives. The plague on Israel did not stop until David, in obedience, bought the threshing floor of Araunah and erected an altar to the Lord. This is the site where God wanted David to locate the Temple for the Lord's name.

Since God picked the time and the place for His Temple in such dramatic fashion, is it possible that this election of Mt. Zion (in 980 BC) corresponds with the return of Mt. Zion in 1967? Let's look at our prophecy block again.

Using the 480 years as a prophecy, we apply the following "rules":

1. Subtract the time of judgment in the desert, 38.6 years
2. Subtract out the part that does not pertain to the subject at issue.

There are some unknown factors involved. We don't know exactly when in 980 BC these events occurred.

But we have good clues. The plague ending the census was at the time of 'wheat threshing' (See I Chronicles 21) so it was about June of 980 BC or -979.7 (lunar) algebraic. David surrendered the throne to Solomon in the late fall of 970 BC, about –969.3 (lunar) so we have a period of harvesting temple building materials of about 10.4 years. Using our 480-year prophecy model we have

```
     481    Years of prophecy
-   38.6    Desert penalty of death
-   10.4    David's years as harvester
-    4.0    Solomon's Reign (that does not pertain to issue)
   427.0
-   x 7[A]  Apply Leviticus 26 and [A]
  2946.0    Years to the actual taking of Temple Mount
-  979.7    Mt. Zion designated
  1966.3    June, 1967!! Retake Mt. Zion
```

The realization that using the 480 years for prophetic analogy and as an analytic prophecy picto-gram is either:

1. Very disturbing, or
2. Very exciting

This is either junk, made monumentous by coincidence, or it is a whole new way of examining Scripture. I'm not suggesting that every day and date be extrapolated indiscriminately, but I know -

With God there are no coincidences!!

God is all knowing and provided this 'history = prophecy' relationship from eternity. The question is: "how do we, as lovers of God's Word, treat these data?"

So far using David's life as a model for end times wars has produced 2009 AD as a date for the Tribulation. This agrees with the extrapolation of Hosea 6.2 for the end of the times of the Gentiles at 2009.

Then using the selection of Mt. Zion in David's life as a Base Point, we also find the extrapolated prophecy for the capturing of Mt. Zion by Israel as 1967 — which did occur in June of 1967!

Are there any other major events milestones or boundaries that are dateable in David's life and also have genuine prophetic correlation and correspondence to events in the future history of Israel?

It seems reasonable to examine David's taking of Jerusalem as a prophetic seed to see if it has correspondence with current/future events.

Jerusalem fell to David's forces some time in 1003 BC. If we assume this was a summer/fall event (as most military adventures are prosecuted in favorable summer weather. Note: a similar reference by the chronologer in I Chronicles 20:1) then we would express this "the fall of 1003 BC" algebraically as - 1002.3. Therefore:

```
      480    Prophecy Block
   -   38.6  Desert penalty to Death (does not apply)
   -    4.0  Solomon's reign (does not apply)
      437.4  Years to apply
    x    7[A]
     3017.8  Years to capture of Jerusalem
   - 1002.3  Initial Taking of Jerusalem (By Jesus via David)
     2015.5  This is Tishri of 2016 (Jesus truly taking Jerusalem)
```

If Jerusalem is "the Great City.... where also their Lord was crucified" in Revelation 11:8 and also seen in Revelation 16:19 (destroyed by the greatest earthquake ever..."the great city split into three parts") then this event of Tishri 2016 is the outpouring of the 7th bowl of God's wrath. After this destruction the next event John relates on earth is Jesus leading the armies of heaven into final victory/conquest over Satan (Revelation 19:11).

[Note: The term 'great city' occurs 10 times in the Revelation. Once it is clearly the holy Jerusalem (21:10), once it is the "the city that reigns over kings of the earth' (17:18). Once it is called the city where the "Lord was crucified" (11:8), once it is unmodified (16:19) and six times it is called Babylon (but not the Babylon of Nebuchadnezzar - that ruin is 250 miles inland and this Babylon can be seen by sailors at sea.) In verses 16:19-20 the earthquake causes *The great city split into three parts, and the cities of the nations collapsed. God remembered Babylon the Great and gave her the cup filled with the wine of the fury of His wrath. Every island fled away and the mountains could not be found."* Though written in highly figurative and symbolic language, verses 19 and 20 seem to indicate that the great earthquake (part of the 7th bowl of God's wrath) which is associated with the return of Jesus (16:15) and the end of the Tribulation will be felt "world-wide". (16:16 is the gathering at Armageddon and 16:17 states, "...*it is done!*") This means that Christ's return will be felt globally - hence "great city" as used in this context is Jerusalem (a place of "good"). The references to nations, cities, Babylon, islands, etc. refer to places of evil and the rest of the world AND its people. The earthquake will be felt everywhere, by everyone.]

If this identification of Jerusalem as the Great City is correct our prediction of Tishri 2016 is in excellent agreement with the rest of the time line events. (The 30 days of Elul (repentance), the sign of the Son of Man, the Harvest, the Judgment and the Wedding Feast. See time line later in this section.)

The year 2016 is generated when we use all of David's reign as pertaining to the 480 year Prophecy block. But what year is presented if we only consider David's warrior years. To examine the warrior years only, we must delete (subtract out) the years as "harvester" of Temple building supplies.

> NOTE: I was not sure if this "approach/technique" was valid but I was astounded at the results. David spent his last years, (from the selection of the altar location at Mt. Zion to the anointing of Solomon) in gathering material for the Temple. This harvesting period was 9.8 years long (from the end of the plague to his death).

The taking of Jerusalem was an historic feat, but the real 'victory' was that at this same time (circa 1002.x) David became king over the tribe of Judah <u>and</u> the tribes of Israel (Northern Tribes). The taking of Jerusalem was with <u>combined arms</u> (with soldiers from both Judah and Israel). In other words, when David (as Jesus) was made the sole king, Israel became a <u>united</u> nation. Israeli <u>Nationhood</u> was thus achieved. This prefigures the prophecy of Hosea 1:11 which says:

> *"The people of Judah and the people of Israel will be reunited, and they will appoint one leader...."*

We will use a date of 1002.75 to approximate the establishment of David as king over all Israel. This value is estimated from 2 Samuel 5:5 which says of David's reign, *"In Hebron he reigned over Judah seven years and six months and in Jerusalem he reigned over all Israel and Judah 33 years."* (KJV)

Since David came to power in 1010 BC, 7 ½ years over Judah would give us until 1002.5. But Solomon's reign starts in 970 BC so David's 33 years began in 1003. For simplicity we set the establishment of David as King of a united Israeli nation at the mid point value of 1002.75 BC. [Note: This is consistent with our previous estimate that Solomon came to the throne in the 9th month (.75 lunar)(see the special note of Chapter 13). Then the calculation yields:

	480	Years of Prophecy
—	38.6	Penalty in Desert
—	9.8	David's Years in Temple Building
—	4.0	Solomon's Reign
	427.6	Years of Prophecy
x	7[A]	
	2950.17	Years to Apply
—	1002.75	Original Israeli Nationhood
	1947.40	**This is the summer of 1948 and Israeli Nationhood!**

Astounding!

The four prophetic events generated by this process are depicted in Figure 14B-2.

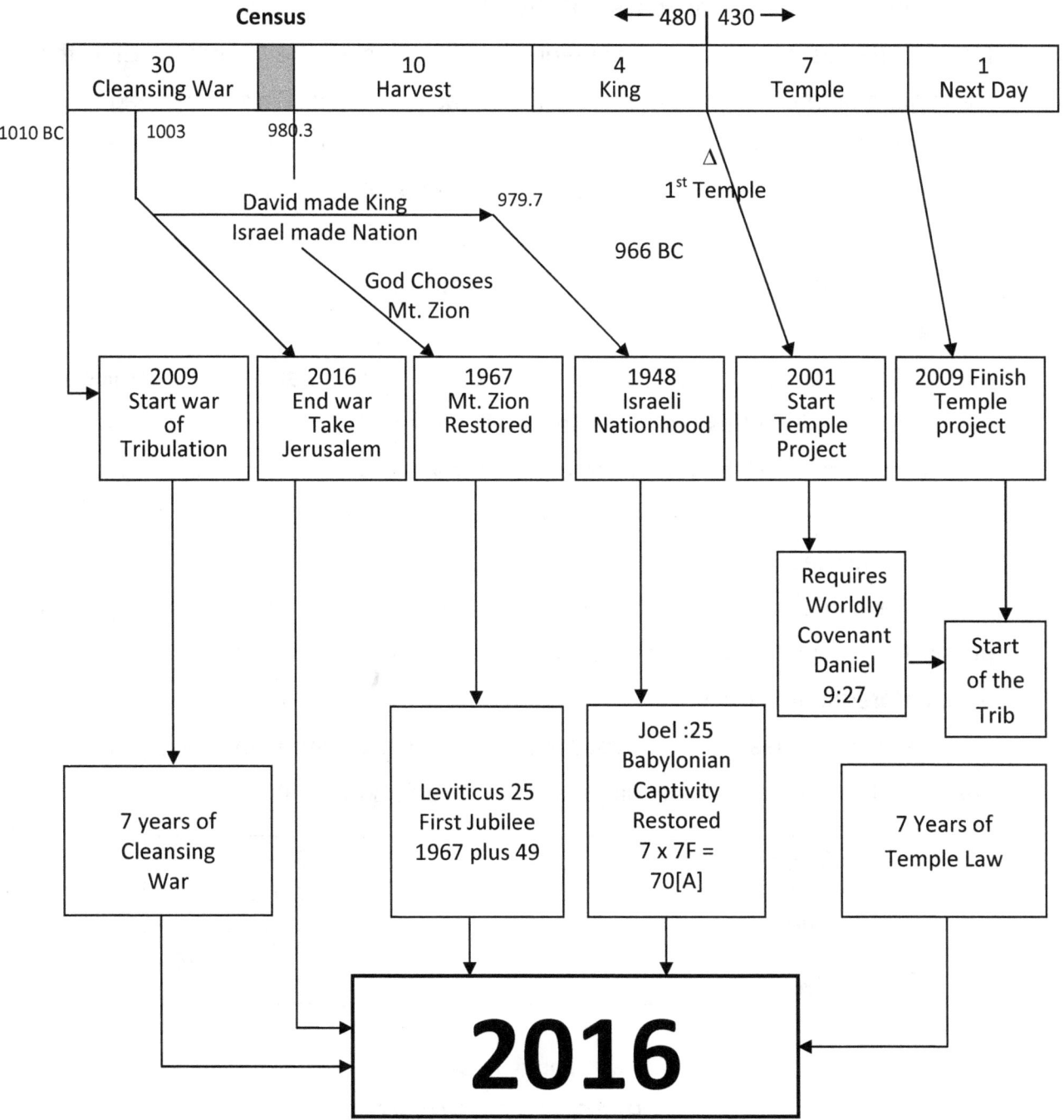

Figure14B-2

THE PROPHECIES OF DAVID'S REIGN

14C   DAVID'S DAYS

It seems clear that the days of David correspond to the cleansing period of the Tribulation. But the number years in each phase of David's life also correspond to the actual "days" of the Second Coming! We begin by letting David's 30 years of warfare represent the 30 days of the month of Elul, the Rabbinic month of Repentance before the feasts of Tishri. This is the beginning of the 40-day season of Teshuvah - the time of repentance (see section on Fall Feasts). This process will <u>start</u> immediately after the Anti-Christ commits the abomination of desolation. This act of abomination is Satan's greatest role-play; the essence of Blasphemy itself, when he declares (in God's own Temple) that he (Satan) is God.

This Satanic act will initiate the sign of the Son of Man and His coming (to the rescue!!). It is at this time that Satan will commit the most vile atrocities in an attempt to destroy all the remaining Jews so that the prophecy of Psalm 110:3

"You will receive the dew of your youth"

cannot be fulfilled. No Jews, no fulfillment!

We can capture some of the spirit of the conflict between Satan and God during the Tribulation by studying the conflict between Pharaoh and God in the days before the first Passover.

Many plagues fell on Egypt but not on God's children who were safe and unaffected in Goshen. These plagues were (See Exodus 7-9):

1. Blood	6. Boils
2. Frogs	7. Hailstones
3. Gnats (or lice)	8. Locusts
4. Flies	9. Darkness
5. Livestock	10. Death

Table 14C-1

PLAGUES OF EGYPT

In general, these plagues repeat themselves during the Tribulation. We see the correlation in the Revelation as follows:

Exodus Plague	In Revelation
Sea into Blood	Revelation 8:8
Frogs of Evil	Revelation 16:13
Gnats(Lice)	{Not mentioned specifically, but referred
Flies	{to as 'pestilence'
Livestock, Famine, Heat	Revelation 16:9, 6:6
Boils, Mark of Beast	Revelation 16:2
Hailstone, Curse God	Revelation 16:21
Locusts, Sting	Revelation 9:3
Darkness	Revelation 8:12

Table 14C-2

PLAGUES OF EGYPT - VS - REVELATION

Finally we come to the ninth plague of the Exodus, the Darkness. This was the last "sign" of God's power before the "death". Let's consider how this plague will repeat as the Sign of the Son of Man approaches. In that day: (Matthew 24:29) "The sun will be darkened and the moon will not give its light"

No Sun Light! No Moonlight! Wow!

No Star Light! WOW!

Just pure blackness for 30 days? Revelation 8:12 speaks of 1/3 of the day turned into darkness. I don't believe this is the whole "darkness" event - no sun, no moon is **NO** light at all.

When you are in an uncomfortable circumstance for ten minutes it can seem like an hour! And an hour of great discomfort can seem like forever. In Exodus, the darkness was for 3 days (clearly a pointer to Jesus who is light. In the Tribulation this darkness will last for 30 days (3x10)) (also a pointer to Jesus who is light). Can you imagine pure fear and terror for 30 days? The utter loneliness! A blackness that separates you from everything physical and leaves you utterly alone with the knowledge of your sins and the <u>sure</u> and <u>certain</u> approach of the wrath of God. All you can see is the Sign of the Son of Man. Pure terror almost unto "death" – which (as plague #10) is guaranteed to follow.

We must also recall here the rescue of Lot and his family from the destruction of Sodom (Genesis 19). The wicked men of Sodom were struck with blindness so that the righteous could walk right past the wicked.

Could this darkness, which precedes the second Coming, be a <u>form</u> of <u>physical</u> blindness that corresponds to the spiritual blindness of the unrepentant heart? How horrible to be suddenly struck blind for 30 days - knowing that judgment was coming upon you and that there was no escape! How helpless and how hopeless - no pride now - just *"moaning and weeping and gnashing of teeth"*.

30 days later, after a period of Great signs in the heavens, the sign of the Son of Man will appear (Note: Just what this "sign" will be is unknown – Jesus' face or maybe a picture of the cross? Who knows? I asked a young girl once who was preparing her heart for the Feast of Trumpets what the sign in the sky could possibly be? She said "His hands" – and that has always seemed as good an answer as I've ever encountered).

Then, after the 30 days of repentance, at the Feast of Trumpets the last 10 days begin and **war outrageous** reigns on the earth. Satan and his millions of 'minions' battle Jesus and all the host of heaven, until at Yom Kippur every knee shall bow and every tongue confesses that Jesus Christ is Lord!

14D SOLOMON'S DAYS

The year/day analogy found in David's reign continues in the reign of Solomon. Following the Judgment Day of Yom Kippur Jesus spends four days in the administration of divine justice. This is seen in Solomon's reign when he spends four years solidifying the throne and his power.

It is during the days of Solomon, when Jesus accepts the crown of Israel, that the righteous coronation of Christ the King is finally accomplished. This is then followed by the changing of garments – a change into the spotless wedding garments of the bride of Christ.

[Note: The "Bride of Christ" analogy has nothing to do with Solomon's many physical marriages. We are speaking about two separate events. The first is the union or solidification of Israel under one unchallenged king. It was during the first four years of his reign that Solomon eliminated all pretenders to the throne. It is during the four days following the 'days of awe' that Jesus will accomplish the commensurate action cleaning out the last trace of royal challenge. The second part of the analogy is obvious - our marriage to the king.]

The significance of a united Israel cannot be overstated. David first brought the tribes into union as Warrior Jesus. (Jesus prays for our oneness - Hosea prophesies it (1:11)) Solomon then maintains this 'marriage' in his 'role' a King of Peace. So Solomon and the four years of his reign that are within this time block (970-966) are also prophecy - of a marriage and a coronation. So when will this coronation/wedding feast begin? Let's look at the 480-prophecy block again. This time we will include the years of Solomon's reign, but omit the period when Israel was not a united nation (while David was king of Judah - 1010 BC to 1002.75).

Therefore:

```
  480.00
 -38.60   Desert Penalty
 - 7.25   Israel as tribes (see prophecy on Nationhood)
  434.15
 x  7[A]
 2995.4   Years to apply
```

Solomon as Jesus: King/Groom begins after the 10 day angelic harvest. This corresponds to the end of the census in our prophecy block – that was Pentecost of 980 or algebraically -979.8. Therefore:

```
 2,995.36
 - 979.80   Pentecost/Mt. Zion end of Census/Harvest
 2015.56    Tabernacles of 2016
```

Here we see that the coronation of Jesus as King of Israel and the marriage feast of the Bride (church) is at the Feast of Tabernacles - the 15th of Tishri through the 21st of Tishri 2016 AD (2015.56).

Now it is time to enter into the millennium. The 1,000 years of peace begins with the first post-Tribulation celebration of the Feast of Tabernacles on the 15th of Tishri – and for seven days the <u>wedding feast is celebrated</u>. (See Figure14D-1.) In the last chapter of Daniel, we find a stunning prophecy on the

Tribulation.

Daniel 12:11, 12 reads:

> *"From the time that the daily sacrifice is abolished and the abomination that causes desolation is set up, there will be 1,290 days. Blessed is the one who waits for and reaches the end of the 1,335 days."*.

We see Satan acting through his agent, the Anti-Christ, taking two distinct actions which mark the last half of the Tribulation. To begin his war on the Jews he "abolishes the daily sacrifice."

This sounds like it is referring to the daily Temple sacrifices that were common to Daniel in his youth. But Daniel made this prophecy toward the end of his life, about 50 years after the Temple of Solomon had been destroyed by Nebuchadnezzar.

So Daniel (like Ezekiel) could see a **future** Temple. Many commentators believe the abominable acts that Daniel foretold referred to the conduct of Antiochus Epiphanes IV who desecrated the second Temple in 167 BC. But we must remember that Jesus refers to this prophecy of Daniel as <u>still in the future</u> (for its final fulfillment).

The great events of the last days
- The sign of the Son of Man
- The Harvest
- The Coronation
- The Wedding Feast
- The Millennial reign

can now be dated and diagrammed (in a time line) by using the reigns of David and Solomon as a prefigured model. Figure 14D-1 is a logical extension of Figure 14B-1 based on this premise.

Daniel tells us that the abomination of desolation - Satan's declaration that he is 'god' - will occur 1290 days after the antichrist stops the daily sacrifice. This event will initiate the visible manifestation of Christ's return - The Sign of the Son of Man. In Figure 14D-1 day 1290 is placed at the beginning of Elul, 30 days before the feast of Trumpets. Daniel also tells us that those who reach day 1335 are "blessed". The 1335th day is 45 days after the 1st of Elul - it is the 15th of Tishri - the feast of Tabernacles - The Wedding Feast. **[Blessed indeed!!!]** Remember God's promise to Abraham: *"...I am... thy exceeding great reward."* (See Genesis 15:1(KJV))

All during the Sign of the son of Man, Satan's wrath will rage against believers, but they are protected by God. Revelation 12:6 tells us that, like the Jews in Goshen, (Exodus 8:22, 9:26) who were safe from the plagues, the Israel of Tribulations (repentant Messiah believes) will be protected 1260 days. This Divine protection ends at the beginning of the Days of Awe - the 1st of Tishri - the Feast of Trumpets - the Harvest. Each heart must now close for Jesus or Satan [Note: In Chapter 17 we will show the redemption of Israel occurs on the 3rd of Tishri during this testing revival.]

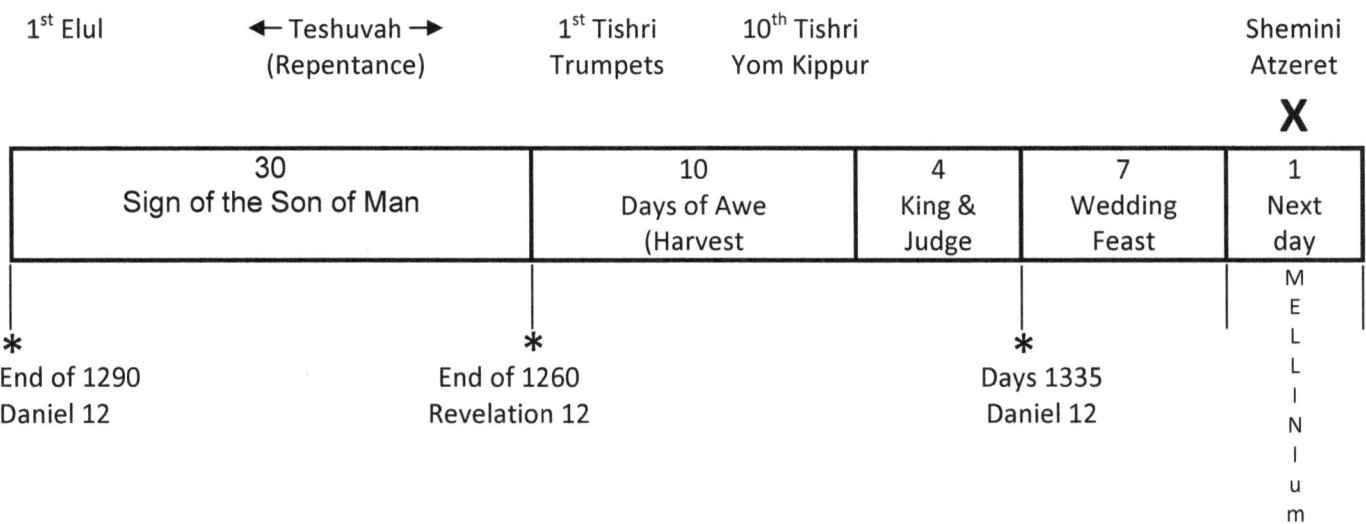

Figure 14D-1
THE LAST DAYS

Jesus links the events of these days to the events of the days of Noah. Well God makes a special covenant with Noah and secures that covenant with a unique prophecy in Genesis 8:22:

> *As long as the earth endures, Seed time and harvest,*
> *Cold and heat, Summer and winter, Day and night,*
> *Will never cease.*

As we have just seen, the end of day and night precede or accompany the sign of the Son of Man which implies to me a deeper additional meaning here – where day and night (and the parallel summer, winter, hot, cold) are references to the cosmic battle of good and evil. Therefore, history is represented by "seed time" and "harvest." Jesus repeatedly compared His gospel to "seed." So dramatic is this picture that all of the Christian era can be thought of as "seed time." Now, with the coming of the Son of Man, the Holy angels will be sent to bring in the "harvest" – this harvest season will last 10 days. (Revelation 2:10)

It was on the 15th day of Tishri that the "Glory of the Lord" entered the first Temple prepared for His name [let it be so with us also – Praise God!!]. As we have seen, the projections in this text indicate that this event will re-occur in 2016.

Let the Jubilee begin! (With a wedding feast - that lasts for seven days!) Note also that Leviticus 23:36 calls for an unnamed celebration on the "eighth" day, the day <u>after</u> Tabernacles ends (since it is held for seven days). This day is called in Hebrew *Shemini Atzeret*: "The Next Day." When we add one more day (signified by the X in our diagram), we clearly see the significance of this new day. It is the day of the millennium (1,000 years) of peace. The 8th day of Tabernacles signifies a new beginning. Here we leave the old behind for good and enter into the next dispensation or age. How do we enter this new age? By holding a sacred assembly and rejoicing with Emmanuel: God with us!!

****

Our study has shown us that the Promised Land was only 1 year away in 1446 BC, but events in real-time ("sin space"?) altered the final length of the salvation history time line. God had no problem inserting 39 years for hard-heartedness in the desert or 2,000 years for the Christian era that we live in (and were "saved" in: Praise God!!).

Has the church done the job that was given her – or like Israel after Joshua, have we failed to proclaim Christ judiciously and **cleanse** our lives appropriately and come out of the world and "be separate"? Or was it just as easy for us to remain in the world, look like the world and seek after the things of this world? Did we thereby abrogate our chance at seeing Jesus in our lifetime? Will God extend "time" again?

I am <u>overcome</u> with the warning Paul gave to the Gentiles, which I paraphrase, "If God grafted you in, He can also graft you out." (Romans 11:21).

> As definitive as the current prophecies appear (5 falling together in 2016 and 2 falling in 2009 (Tribulation), God is still not "forced" to call an end to this mysterious "salvation process". **He may "insert" yet another "AGE"** for our blessing and growth.

15.0 SEGMENT PROPHECY BLOCK 430

15A ALL OVER AGAIN

When Moses and all Israel left Egypt, they traveled 50 days to Mt. Sinai. When Moses and all Israel left Mt. Sinai, it was the 20th of Ziv 1445 BC. They reached the entrance to the Promised Land when it was "the season for the first ripe grapes," or about the 1st of Ab (the 5th month) (or about June). This trip from law to land (from regulation to rest) was only 40 days. Had Moses just plunged right in, the trip would have been over in a month and a half. The kingdom would be now! But he didn't! He and all Israel did "flesh" things: scouting parties, spies, meetings, reports, etc. So God made a 40-day trip into a 40-year journey.

When Joshua entered the land he knew Israel had a fight on their hands. But the Lord would fight for Israel (if they wanted Him). Israel tried to do some fighting on their own and slowed the whole cleansing process down. And when Joshua died, Judah (the Tribe), the next leader, (after Caleb) chose to "love their neighbor" rather than fight. So they settled down and with pagans and married with the world and its gods. This period from Joshua to David was 390 years (the sin of the House of Israel). (The use here for "House of Israel" refers to the whole nation, not just the northern tribes.) And because Judah was the recalcitrant leader, the additional penalty of 40 years (the Sin of the House of Judah) fell to David. If we <u>remove</u> this period of disobedience, we get the **adjusted** chronology seen in Figure 15A-1.

We see here that without this sin, the promised land, the Kingdom of God (and His Rest), would have been reached in the <u>Jubilee</u> of their freedom. Forty years marching and ten years cleaning (6 years for Joshua and 4 years for Solomon). Solomon's Temple foundation (laid in his fourth year) is an <u>Ebenezer</u> to this milestone. Here is a picture of Jesus' Kingdom arriving 50 years after Israel's freedom, which we will discuss again in Chapter 16 (God is not slow to keep his promises as some men count slowness). (See 2 Peter 3:9)

We can now understand Jesus' remark to the Pharisee during the triumphal entry that if the people were quiet, *"even the stones would cry out."*

That is their job!! They were an Ebenezer. They were placed there by Solomon as a testimony of the Kingdom. These stones are a witness of the first **missed** Jubilee – the Jubilee that should have been, had the process gone God's way.

The first time God tried to bring His children home was with Moses. The Kingdom was only 50 days from Sinai – (See Appendix 5) Now this second time, it took 50 years to the Ebenezer (another example of the day/year penalty process) and the real kingdom was still not secure.

How could those old stones have kept quiet when they saw Jesus coming! A witness long silent - they would gladly rejoice and sing out:

"HAIL TO THE KING!"

40	+	6	+	4	= 50
Moses		Joshua		Solomon	

Δ
Foundation I

Figure 15A-1
FIRST JUBILEE

It is interesting to note that when Israel refused the Kingdom the first time (after the 40 day exploration), they had been on their journey 17 months. How many years is this? Seventeen months divided by 12 months per year equals $\frac{17}{12} = 1.42$ years of free will obedience.

If we multiply this "travel time" by 7 we get: 1.42 x 7 = 9.94 years

This is the 10-year period of Joshua and Solomon together. God punished the hard-hearted people of Moses' day with death and denial ("they shall not enter my rest"), but the Nation and it's journey **also suffered** since their "travel time" is multiplied by 7. This is the first use of Leviticus 26:18, 21 on our journey to "Kingdom Come." We will see this multiplier used often.

> [NOTE: The Anderson coefficient may be present here since 17/12 x 7 = 10 prophetic years which would be realized in the 9.94 earth years (10[A] = 9.94).Unfortunately, the dates are not definitive enough to discern the presence of the Anderson operator, e.g., we do not know on exactly what date the spies gave the rejection report. But there is a strong hint of this

coefficient's first presence in the history/time adjustment].

Now if the first application of Leviticus 26:18, 21 produced 1.42 x 7 ≈ 10 years, is it reasonable that the next application of this divine factor would produce 10 x 7 = 70 years? Oh, Yes! This is where our story started with the "why 70 years?" for the prophecy of Jeremiah. Yes, 70 years is required by the laws of Sabbath rest, but also by Leviticus 26:18, 21 and the rules for recurring sin.

Well, the next multiplier would be 70 x 7 = 490. Wow! This is the prophecy of Daniel on the end of days. We see in the 70 years of Jeremiah what might be called a "re-take" (or as little kids, we called it a "do-over"). In other words, "try again." God physically removes the Israelites from the Kingdom and ships them back to Egypt (Babylon), destroys the Temple (the first Jubilee marker), and says okay, try again–and get it right this time!

The destruction of the Babylonian empire in 538 BC was the equivalent of the devastation of Egypt at the time of the plagues – both captivities ended without the Jews "firing a shot." The Persian King Cyrus, the prophesied servant of the Lord (see Isaiah 45:13) conquers Babylon by stealth, not strength, and sets the Jews free for another desert journey. But it's not two million sojourners this time. Only 50,000 - perhaps. They reach Jerusalem by Tishri of 537 BC.

It is notable that Tishri is the month in which Jubilee begins. The fall feasts of 537 BC commemorate another Jubilee – the return to Jerusalem occurred on the 49th year anniversary of the city's and the Temple's destruction. (The start of the 50th year.) But there is also a true heavenly Jubilee here. God has cleansed His Holy Hill – the giants that Israel would not address in Numbers 13 have been eradicated - recall how severe Ezra was in the area of foreign marriage (Ezra 9 & 10). The Jews were to be separate, clean, Holy unto God.

The Jews' trip home is also noteworthy. Remember Moses and the 1.5 years that failed (see Chapter 12). Here we see that our first suspicion was correct. The period for worship required 3 days - 1½ days out and 1 ½ days back. But via the day/year relationship this became one and a half years. The second trip home out of Egypt (Babylon) takes just 1.5 years (Nisan '38 to Tishri '37). The Jews succeed the second time, thereby insuring the 1.5 days – 1500 years glory of that God intended – 1500 years in the Kingdom. (1500 [A] from first Passover to Jesus).

In the spring of 536 BC, the émigrés laid the foundation of the second Temple –the second Ebenezer to the Kingdom. **Also a failed jubilee.** When the second Temple is finally finished, the Shikina Glory of God **does not** return to the Holy of Holies. Despite the heroic efforts of these first settlers, the Nation of Israel will remain under judgment. They have been granted a second chance, but along with that grace, there is a period of parole or probation – 360 years remain on the original 430-year sentence (See Ezekiel 4:5, 6).

It is during the Jews' journey home that the prophet Daniel, while still in Babylon, receives his vision of the seventy-sevens. The exiles are not even home yet and the next pronouncement of the "time delay" for the coming of the Kingdom is given from Heaven. (The Jews still have one year left to serve on the old (current) sentence). But God has had enough of this fooling around, wandering in the desert, trying to find the way (the Way) to the Kingdom. God announces that He will send His only begotten Son to lead the nation into the Kingdom [He knows the Way]. And this will happen precisely 490 prophetic years after the Jews build a wall around Jerusalem (**i.e., become "separate"**!!).

It seems quite significant that this announcement is given while "the Nation" is still in Egypt – no one is in Israel (Jerusalem/**rest**). At the time of the pronouncement, Jerusalem is a "desolate sanctuary" (Daniel 9:17). It will take Jesus to lead "the Nation" to this Jerusalem – to this **rest**. This is very significant because it is the wall around Jerusalem that symbolically makes Israel (Jerusalem) separate from the world - hence: reserved, dedicated, and consecrated wholly to God.

NOTE: In Nehemiah 2:20 – Nehemiah, speaking for all Israel, declares to the non-believers (the world) about the wall building project and the City of Jerusalem.

> *"We, His servants, will start rebuilding, but as for you–*
> *You have no share in Jerusalem ..."*

Nehemiah had great spiritual help in his wall-building project. That help came from Daniel who prayed for the desolate city - about 100 years earlier.

Notice in Daniel 9:17 that Daniel prays for the city of Jerusalem and is given an immediate double answer: 1) Yes, your people will return to the city because 2) they will receive a decree to rebuild the walls and the streets.

God answers Daniel's prayer in part because Daniel understands from Scripture and <u>believes</u> the 70 years are ended. Daniel sees through the eyes of faith and feels Nehemiah's pain (see Nehemiah 1) and the pain of all the believers caused by the desolation of the city.

Daniel's one prayer for Jerusalem's renewal generates two decrees:

    A.   538 BC, Cyrus' decree sends the Jews home to rebuild the Temple.

    B.   445 BC, Artaxerxes' decree sends Nehemiah home to rebuild the city and its walls.

So we see that <u>BOTH</u> decrees (Cyrus' decree that set the Jews free and Artaxerxes' decree to rebuild the wall) are given in response to Daniel's prayer. These edicts are therefore linked together like 'one thing' or 'one decree' in a prophetic prayer -space. But this prayer is issued and answered (in part) during the 430-year sin penalty, specifically during the last year of the 70-year captivity. The prophetic answer to Daniel's prayer spiritually linked the return of the Jews to Jerusalem with the coming of the Anointed One: It is Messiah, Jesus, who would guide the believers into the true Jerusalem. (This scenario will be replayed quite soon – Praise God!). This overall process is shown in Figure 15A-2.

It is **extreme irony** that the walls of Daniel 9:27 that "separated" Jewish believers from the world (and sin) brought salvation to the rest of the world. Upon the rejection of Jesus inside the walls, he is crucified <u>outside</u> those walls, amid the people that Nehemiah 2:20 says "have no part in Jerusalem." (This also fulfills Matthew 21:39, outside the vineyard). So Jesus was given to those beyond the walls – the Gentiles! Praise God!! [Thereby fulfilling Yahweh's promise to Abraham - "and <u>all peoples</u> of the earth will be blessed through you" Genesis 12:3c .]

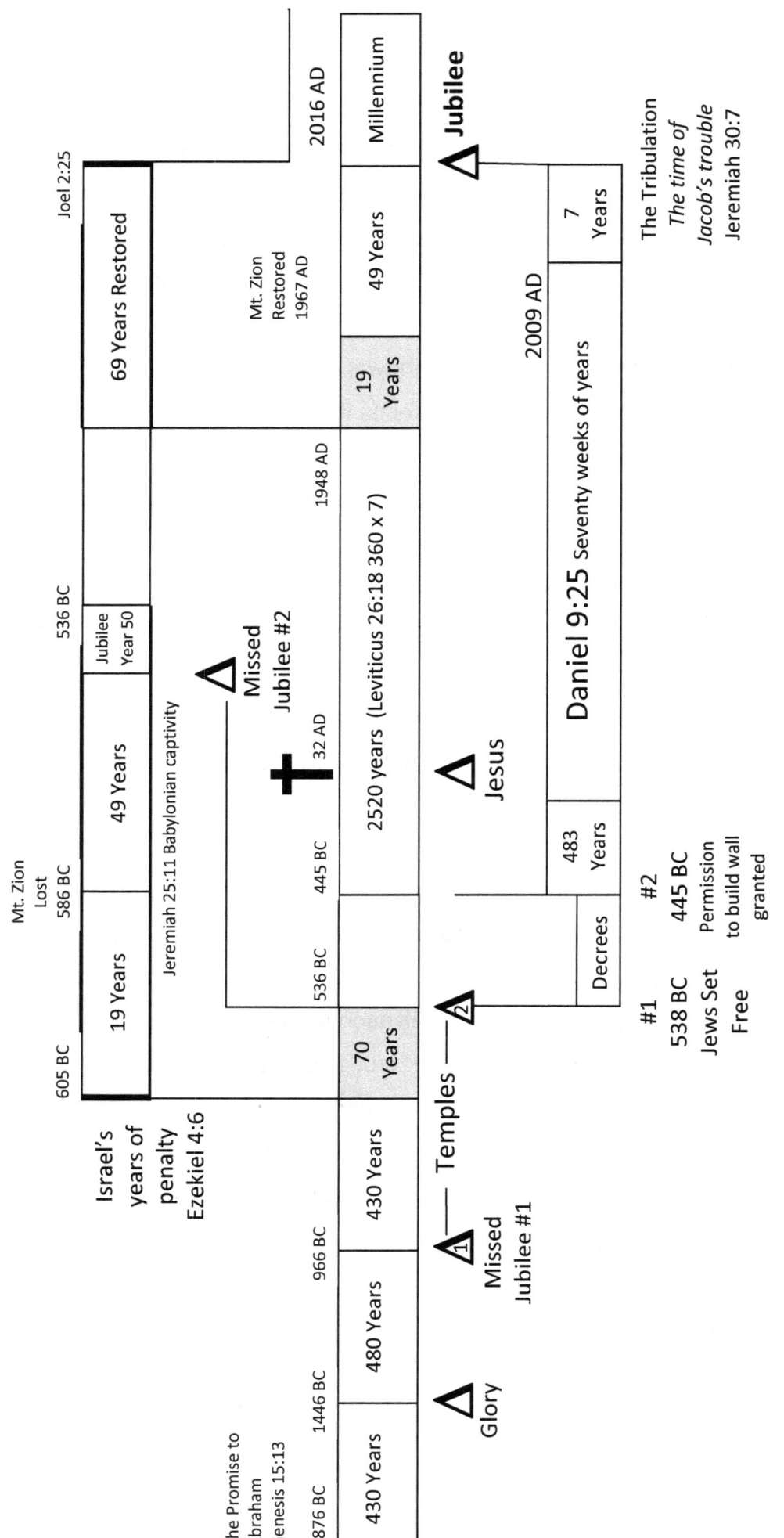

Figure 15A-2
Salvation's Prophecy Space

15B   MEANING AND PROPHECY

After finding striking prophecy in the 480 year "cleansing" period, I was sure even more wonders would be found in the 430 year "sin" period, but I was in for a surprise.

The game here is not to run hither and yon multiplying every fig leaf by 7[A] and driving a solution from hindsight, for which I'm afraid I was most guilty. The blocks of years can't be forced out of character. They represent a distinct flavor and carry a specific message which must be first understood in context. For the 480-year period, it was obvious. It was war - the annihilation of God's enemies – kind of. The greater message however, is that the chosen people were given the task of "cleansing" but rather chose "mixing" so that the work of separation and cleansing must eventually be done by God Himself. We Christians, having been reborn in God's spirit, should be very sensitive to the separation issue. 1 Peter says in 2:9:

> "But you are a chosen people, a royal priesthood, a Holy nation, a people belonging to God." (KJV)

Sadly, <u>we are not</u> very sensitive to the separation issue. And neither was Israel – She intermarried with the world and accepted the world's gods. For the most part so have we Christians, but that is another story. The acceptance of the world (a pagan world and pagan values) caused the lack of separation for 390 years. Forty more years were for Judah's lack-luster leadership hence 430 years of total sin penalty.

So the block of 430 years must have the message rightly divided in order to glean the prophetic direction. Since Solomon's Temple (a clear sign of millennium) initiates the period, I was convinced that all sorts of second coming references could be found. But once you identify the message of the block, you must also find the future period that corresponds to this message. Then, if you're so fortunate, you must also match singular historic events in the block that require prophetic fulfillment with their future counterpart. All this symbolic matching must <u>come first</u>, and then we can look for day/year correlation.

The 430-year period does start in magnificence, but it turns out to be a replay of the Garden of Eden story. Solomon dies and two rivals (Rehoboam and Jeroboam) split the kingdom, consider killing each other, propose open warfare (stopped by God), and finally, settle on divorce (you be Israel and I'll be Judah). ["I hate divorce," says the Lord God…Malachi 2:16] So God, with a punishment that fit the crime, (the God who would have been Israel's chief warrior in driving enemies from the land), **brings enemies against Israel**. God strengthens those enemies and uses them **to destroy the divorced**. [NOTE: Another deep message in the 480-year period is a by-product of separation (from the world) and that message is "union" (into true Israel). The twelve tribes had to come together to become one people – one heart. (This took the spirit of Jesus as represented by David/Solomon). What God required of His first born, He also requires of us, His adopted. Jesus prays that we will be "one" and Paul reminds us sharply to be of one body, one mind and one spirit].

Israel and Judah, who would not fight together for God, ended up fighting alone – against God. They became the "enemy" that was cleansed from the land and scattered to the wind. ["Rejecters be gone!"]

> *"Then the Lord said, 'call him Lo-Ammi, for you are not my people and I am not your God'"* (Hosea 1:9)

The Land was cleansed.

But He reminds us (Hosea 6:2)

> *"After two days he will revive us*
> *On the third day he will restore us,*
> *that we may live in His presence."*

(Hosea 2:23)

> *"I will plant her for myself in the land;*
> *and I will show my love to the one I called 'not my loved one.'*
> *I will say to those called 'Not my people', 'You are my people'; and they will say,* **"You are my God"**.

And again (Hosea 1:11)

> *"The people of Judah and the people of Israel will be* **reunited,** *and they will appoint* **one leader** *and will come up out of the land, for great will be the day of Jezreel."*

So block 430 does not show us the millennia utopia as I presupposed. Rather, it shows war and defeat of those (even His own) who oppose God's will. Since all of block 430 is history under judgment, we have no select pieces to exclude. The 70 years captivity and return remain in the history block while the residual 360 x 7 forms the next period of history.

But let's focus on that point in the period where Israel **is** performing God's will -during the construction of the first Temple. The Temple was completed during the 11th year of Solomon's reign in the month of Bul the eighth month of 959 BC. Therefore:

```
      430
    x   7[A]
   2966.7    years of delay to the "true Temple"
   - 958.3   completion of Temple 8th month of 959
   2008.4    Hebrew calendar

   2008.4    Start of Trib about Elul of 2009
   +   7.0   End of Trib
   2015.4    Start of "true Temple" about Elul 2016
```

[Note: The decimal value .4 is June if we use a solar calendar, but these are Hebrew - lunar calendar predictions (God's calendar - feast calendar). The end of .4 therefore, is the start of the period of repentance, Teshuvah, which begins with the month of Elul and initiates the sign of the son of Man and Glory!!!]

The most significant feature of the period, the construction of Solomon's Temple, is used by God as a marker that points to the main message of the 430-year period God's final cleansing of the land. Then, once the land is cleansed, the "true Temple", the Glory of the Lord Himself arrives!! (Praise God!)

The other significant date in the 430-year block is the very day the period starts, in the second month, Ziv 966, the foundation of the first Temple. Therefore,

$$\begin{array}{r} 430 \\ \times 7[A] \\ \hline 2966.7 \\ -965.9 \text{ Start Temple} \\ \hline 2000.8^2 \end{array}$$

The obvious future parallel to the start of Solomon's Temple is the start of the future Temple (the third Temple) wherein Satan, through the Anti-Christ, will commit the abomination of desolation.

It was previously speculated that the permission to build that Temple might be part of the 'covenant' that begins the Tribulation. But our previous calculations put the start of the Tribulation in 2009. If that is so, what is the significant counter-part to this date in early 2001 AD? Will an attempt to start Temple construction cause major trouble for Israel? Will this begin the period of trouble that allows the anti-Christ to rise to the forefront as a supposed 'peace maker'. We will soon see.

[Note: Do any of our readers see a clear correlation with these prophetic projections?]

---

[2] .8 is on the lunar calendar. This is almost ten months after Easter of 2000. That's about January of 2001, which is the beginning of the third Christian Millennium.

16.0 GOD CALCULUS

16A THE PENALTY BRICK

When the Jews rejected the land, the Promised Land, God penalized them one-year delay for each day of exploration. They got 40 years. (Peter also gives us the day to a thousand years metric). We need to look at that 40-year period closely.

When the Jews left Egypt, they went 50 days to Mt. Sinai and received the Law. They camped at Sinai for about a year and then headed toward the target – the Promised Land. Well, they scouted the Promised Land for 40 days, starting "at the season of the first ripe grape harvest." (Good clue, good clue!) In general, the first ripe grape harvest is around the first part of the 4th month, the month of Tammuz. Forty days later brings disaster!! You know the rest of the story. The 40-year "judgment" does not end until the "change unto God" is complete and all the old generation is dead. Thus a new and cleansed generation enters the land (on the 10th of Nisan 1406 BC).

We might look at this period graphically as

The "F" represents the period of "free choice" unto God prior to the rejection of the Promised Land. (The term "free choice" might also be considered the "free will" portion). And the penalty, or "P", portion is the time from the rejection of the land to the death of the adults. (Reject God = death! That sounds like a valid rule!). If we try to estimate how long these periods were, we only have one clue – that it was "time for the first ripe grape harvest." Well that's about the start of month 4 on the lunar calendar, or mid-June by our calendar. Forty days later would be about the middle to the end of month 5. Therefore, the freewill period was about 1 year and 4½ to 5 months long.

We don't know if year 1446 BC had a "second Adar" so the point of rejection was **about** 11½ months (first year) plus 4½ months (second year) to

12½ months (first year) to 5 months (second year), or 16 to 17½ months. We will use 17 and work from there! Thus:

$$F = \frac{17}{12} = 1.42 \text{ years}$$

If F = 1.4 years, then:

$$P = 40 - F = 38.6 \text{ years}$$

So the time spent waiting for death was 38.6 years – so what! Who cares? Well, let's see where this goes.

When Moses sent spies into the land, what was their task? What assessment were they making? They were <u>assessing</u> the task of "cleansing the land."

Spiritually this is the task of repentance and separation. This cleansing leads to holiness and holiness to rest, Kingdom, Jesus! Cleaning house! Getting sin out of our lives and <u>separating</u> – keeping sin out of our lives.

Well Israel said there were <u>giants</u> in the land!! There was BIG SIN in their hearts/lives – too much world, too much to give up – the price was too high (thank God Jesus paid the price!).

[NOTE: When David took up the challenge of cleansing the land he had to begin with the old, left-over giants (Goliath, et al.), then he could get on with the rest of the cleansing program!]

Israel wasn't chosen by God to be an "assessment maker". Israel wasn't set free – taken out of bondage – in order to "report and evaluate". Israel was chosen by God to make His name great and Israel was set free to clean and to claim the land – the "Holy" land – unto God!

The first mission was a complete failure – the penalty was death. <u>Repent or perish</u>! Sounds familiar! Jesus said that too! The journey to this "Holy land" was "delayed." The "delay" lasted until the sin clock and the penalty clock both ran to zero – this took forty years – forty years for "change unto God." Once this point was reached, once the penalty was paid (death!), and then the journey continued. Now God would deal with the "free will" portion of the next generation.

This generation would also fail in the free will portion of the test. More penalties were added. When we look at these cases carefully, we see some of the mathematics of God.

There "appears" to be an interesting relation between "F" and the lengths of time delays we see in Scripture. If we multiply "F" (=1.42) by seven (7) we find:

$$F \times 7 \approx 10 \text{ years}$$

Recall that the cleansings of Joshua and Solomon together were 10 years. The 40-year wandering plus the 10-year cleansing of the land made a 50-year Jubilee (the foundation of the first Temple). Let's see how close our original estimate for "F" was.

We said "F" was 1.42 years. But 7 x 1.42 = 9.94 years. That's close to ten years but not <u>real</u> close. But remember, when we are talking about prophetic time and real time, we need to include the Anderson's coefficient [A] = (360/365.25).

When we do this, things look a might better.

$$\frac{F \times 7}{[A]} = \frac{1.42 \times 7}{[A]} = 10.08 \text{ years}$$

[Note: We usually multiply our prophetic years by [A] to get real years. Here we are looking for the number of prophetic years, so we divide by [A].]

A discrepancy of 8 parts in a thousand is still too large. Is there a less subjective methodology we can use to solve for "F"?

16B FREEWILL RELATIONS

We might remember that the exile period for Israel to meditate on her national spiritual values was 70 prophetic years. Israel needed to "clean house" and start over so God gave them "seven times greater" opportunity than Joshua/Solomon to do this. But they failed miserably. The 430-year sin period following Solomon's reign was filled with chaos, pride, throne wars, and selfishness...a nation gone totally worldly. You may recall the words of Jesus about how bad (incomplete) housecleaning will result in a 7 times penalty. (This clearly shows us the "how" and the "why" on a national, historic time scale.) (See Luke 11:26)

An ideal case for "F", therefore, could be written:

$$7 \times (7 \times F) = 70$$

When we add Anderson's coefficient [A] to the equation to get real years, we have

$$7 \times (7 \times F) = 70[A] \approx 69$$

actual years of penalty (605BC - 536 BC)

Remember how Daniel's prophecy of Jesus was commensurate with the release of Israel from captivity? Israel remained on probation but the true cleansing, the Tribulation, was coming. Daniel's vision of the Messiah was also the vision of the true cleansing – the end times. How long until God did this cleansing Himself? 490 years?

Now we can write an absolute expression containing "F":

$$7 \times 7 \times (7 \times F) = 490 \text{ Prophetic Holy Years.}$$

When we included calculations with [A], we saw that the results for Jesus' arrival (the triumphal entry) were correct to the day. Applying [A] to our absolute case gives us:

$$7^3 F = 490[A]$$

$$(343) \times (1.41) = (490) \times \left(\frac{360}{365.2425}\right)$$

$$483.63 \neq 482.96$$

HELP!!!

They don't match – what's wrong? Our guess for "F" that was based on the grape harvest! Remember we chose 17 months or 1.42 years. Now we can solve for "F":

$$7^3 F = 482.96$$

$$F = (482.96)/343$$

$$\boxed{F = 1.408 \text{ years}}$$

Our approximation for F = 1.42, was very close. F = 1.408 is better.

16C   REJECT GOD = DEATH

The destruction of the Temple on 9 Ab 70 AD has been used in this text as the end of Law (until the Trib).

Jesus prophesied the devastation that befell Jerusalem because:"You didn't recognize the time of your visitation". We have looked at great moments in time when Israel was asked to put down the old and take up the new. Great moments when major "cleansing" was required. Accepting Jesus as Messiah was an "out with the old - in with the new" opportunity. This is certainly one of the <u>great</u> moments in Jewish history. To **test** the theory of this work, let's use the end of Law penalty/judgment to see if it matches the models developed here. (If it truly is God's calculus, it will work perfectly!) We are at a boundary between Law and Grace similar to the boundary in Exodus between slavery and Law. If Jesus is the King of the Jews, the Son of God, will the Jews finally repent of Egypt and accept their King and thereby enter into their rest? They will if they accept the new wine. Only if they accept Jesus.

The penalty faced by Moses and his people for having such hard hearts was death. We see the same general format here – the Jews reject Jesus and "die in their sins" – the Temple is destroyed, the people are scattered across the face of the earth. [Major mistake!] This penalty phase unto death did take **about** 38+ years. It ended on 9 Ab 70 AD. Exactly 40 years earlier would have been 9 Ab 30 AD. If the math analysis in this work is right and this penalty to Israel is **identical** to the one given to Moses's people, then at plus 1.408 years [the period of free will (F)] we will find the <u>key</u> sin – **the sin unto death = the rejection of God!** The Old Testament Jews rejected God's gift of the kingdom…will the Jews of the New Testament reject God's gift of Jesus?

Okay, let's test our theory.

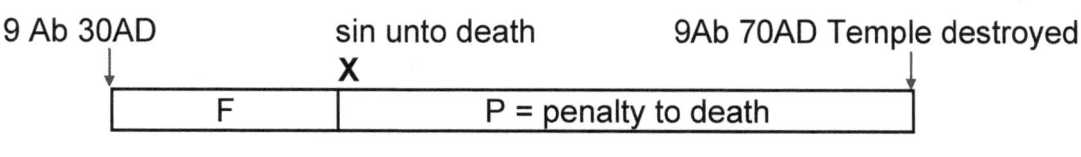

Figure 16C-1
TEST BRICK

TEST: From Figure 16C-1 and using the rules of penalty and prophecy developed in this text we are challenged to find out:

1. The date of X in Figure 16C-1 (recall that F = 1.408).
2. The event in Israel's history and Jesus' life that marks this major milestone.
3. The sin unto death of the Jews

Step 1. Let's find out what the date of the crucifixion was [this seems like a good "key" event to try first]. Since the crucifixion was on the 14th of Nisan 32 AD:

14 Nisan 32 is two weeks after New Years or 31AD + 2/52

thus

Crucifixion = 31.038 AD

Step 2. Let's find out when our starting point 9 Ab 30 is?

Ab is the fifth month so using the Hebrew calendar:

	Month	Days
1.	Nisan	30
2.	Ziv	29
3.	Sivan	30
4.	Tammuz	29
5.	Ab	9
	Total =	127 days

9 Ab is 127 days into the new year. Then 9 Ab 30 AD would be the year 29 + 127 days or:

$$29 + \frac{127}{365} = 29.348$$

Thus

9 Ab 30 = 29.348 AD

Step. 3 Are these the dates of our "F" period boundaries?
Let's subtract the start date from the crucifixion date.

    Crucifixion = 31.038
    9 Ab 30 = 29.348 (start of 40 years)
    Difference = 1.690 (years to crucifixion)

Step. 4 Since F = 1.408, the difference found in step 3 of 1.690 years is <u>too large</u>, the crucifixion **was not** the key date in Jewish history!

How much <u>earlier</u> than the crucifixion was this key date?? Subtract the dates!

    + 1.690 years to crucifixion
    - 1.408 length of "F"

Therefore   .282 years too long.

The key sin date was .282 years **before** the crucifixion of Jesus. (See Figure 16C-2)

Figure 16C-2
KEY DATE BEFORE CRUCIFIXION

Step. 5   How many days before the crucifixion is .282 years?
.282 x 365 = 103 days
103 is 3½ months earlier than crucifixion (14 Nisan)

or:

Month	Days
Nisan	14
Adar	29
Shebat	30
Tebeth	29
Kislev	1
total =	103 days

Thus 103 days **prior** to the crucifixion was the last day of Kislev. That night is the New Moon Festival to begin the month of Tebeth. Thus it is the 1st of the 10th month.

Step 6. Can we identify what Jesus was doing on this day – Yes!!! **Incredibly**, Yes!!!

It was the New Moon Festival that was part of the Feast of the Dedication. It was the major winter feast of Chanukah – the Second Festival of Lights – which celebrated the Maccabean victory of 165 BC – **the rededication of the Temple**.

On this very day of re-dedication, God was asking Israel to **rededicate to Jesus**. Look at John 10:22-39 especially verse 30

22 And it was at Jerusalem the feast of the dedication, and it was winter. 23 And Jesus walked in the Temple in Solomon's porch. 24 Then came the Jews round about him, and said unto him, How long dost thou make us to doubt? If thou be the Christ, tell us plainly. 25 Jesus answered them, I told you, and ye believed not: The works that I do in my Father's name, they bear witness of me. 26 But ye believe not, because ye are not of my sheep, as I said unto you. 27 My sheep hear my voice, and I know them, and they follow me: 28 And I give unto them eternal life; and they shall never perish, neither shall any man pluck them out of my hand. 29 My Father, which gave them me, is greater than all; and no man is able to pluck them out of my Father's hand. ***I and my Father are one. 31****Then the Jews took up stones again to stone him. 32 Jesus answered them, Many good works have I shown you from my Father; for which of those works do ye stone me? 33 The Jews answered him, saying****, For a good work we stone thee not; but for blasphemy; and because that thou, being a man, makest thyself God.*** *34 Jesus answered them, Is it not written in your law, I said, Ye are gods? 35 If he called them gods, unto whom the word of God came, and the Scripture cannot be broken; 36 Say ye of him, whom the Father hath sanctified, and sent into the world, Thou blasphemest; because I said, I am the Son of God? 37 If I do not the works of my Father, believe me not. 38 But if I do, though ye believe not me, believe the works: that ye may know, and believe, that the Father is in me, and I in him. 39 Therefore they sought again to take him: but he escaped out of their hand…* (KJV)

Step. 7   What was the key sin? See John 10:33

"We are not stoning you for any of these (miracles)", replied the Jews, "but for blasphemy, because you, a mere man, claim to be God." (KJV)

The only sin unto death is blasphemy! The blasphemy of the Holy Spirit – rejecting Jesus as the Son of God. On this very day the Jews, as a nation, committed this offense - **38.6 years later the nation suffers death.**

So Jesus leaves the Temple and <u>does not return</u> (i.e. the Jews have made their decision!) until it is time – until the hour of the Son of Man has reached the

appointed (Mo`ed) time for the Son of God to become the **Lamb** of God who stands inspection for 4 days in the Temple and is then slain – for you and me!

Praise God!

16D   THE 7 YEAR MIRACLE

The death of Jesus of Nazareth closed the sixty-ninth week of the prophecy of Daniel. Ten days after Jesus' ascension into heaven, the gift of the Holy Spirit fell upon the church. The gospel of the resurrected Messiah was preached throughout Israel – thousands of Jews were saved. The church of Jesus the Christ was a Jewish church filled with Torah observant, Torah knowledgeable, Torah believing Jews. They knew the prophecies of Daniel.

They knew the "time of Jacob's trouble" was imminent. Even the non-Christian Jews realized it was time for Messiah and then the end of the age. They could count 483 years or so back to Nehemiah (and Artaxerxes). And God was faithful to His word. Even though 2000 prophetic years of grace have been inserted in the time line of Salvation, the end of the age did come right on time! We read in Acts 10 of Peter's laying hands on Cornelius (a Gentile). And the Gift of God – the Spirit of Jesus – went out to the Gentile world. This happened in 38 AD. That means that God gave the Jews of Jesus' day seven years of the Holy Spirit. To those who believed, Life; to those who did not believe, the penalty unto death was served. At a time when first Century students of prophecy were expecting the end of time – calamity, disaster and ruin – God fulfilled the schedule (in a manner of speaking) with the end of the age...the end of the age of Law and the beginning of the age of Grace. At a time when a wrathful God could have been more than justified in destroying Israel for the rejection and death of His only Son – God miraculously provided the gift of the Holy Spirit. The diagram in Figure 16D-1 helps illustrate the insertion of the 7-year miracle of the Holy Spirit and the re-positioning of Daniel's 70th week (the Tribulation) until the end of the age of grace (and the renewing of Law). (See Figure 16D-1)

The age of grace = 2000 [A] is 1971 years duration by this prophetic approach. Beginning in 38 AD, it would end, baring any new agenda by God, in the year 2009. [38 + 1971 = 2009] At this point, the 7-year Tribulation would begin. The age of Law would return and this period of wrath would climax with Jesus' return in the fall of 2016.

Praise God!

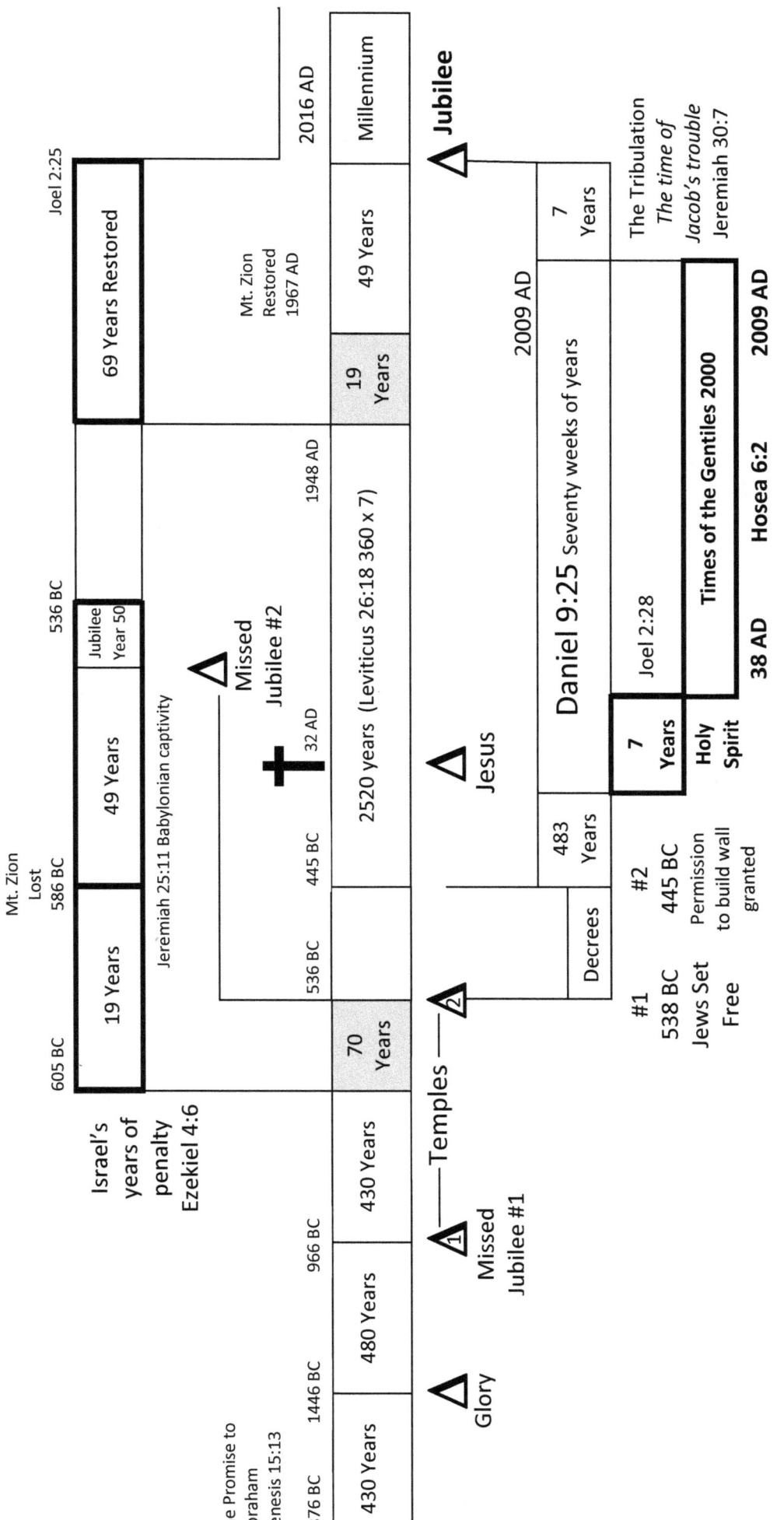

Figure 16D-1
7-YEAR MIRACLE

17.0 Promises, Promises

17A Days of Noah

God's holy promise that a Redeemer would come (...and come again) is seen throughout the Old Testament. The pledge to restore fallen creation is older than Adam's exile. For God says to Satan:

> "...I will put enmity between thee and the woman, and between thy seed and her seed; it shall bruise they head, and thou shalt bruise his heel." Genesis 3:15 (KJV)

This "seed", this redeemer, is also found in God's covenant with Noah. After the flood God promises to never destroy the world by water again. The surety for this pledge is given in Genesis 8:22:

> "As long as the earth endures
> seedtime and harvest,
> cold and heat, summer and winter,
> day and night
> will never cease."

Since Jesus is The Word and The Word is 'seed', could the length or duration of "seedtime" be contained in the story of Noah and the events of the flood?

Note: It was the data contained in the flood narrative that provided Sir Robert Anderson with the first clues to the nature of God's clock. With these clues Anderson was able to solve the prophecy of Daniel's 70 sevens.

We have repeatedly seen God orchestrate the events of history to reflect the Glory of His Son. This is also true for the flood events – they too give the story of Jesus. Note that we are not given any narrative about the flood – no tidal wave inundation stories or Hollywood special effects. We know nothing about life on the ark or what went on from day to day. Why? Because the message – the greater message – is "the calendar". The Holy Spirit was explicit in recording the very dates and segment durations of the flood events. Why? Because these dates and lengths prophesy and glorify Jesus. Figure 17-1 illustrates the significant dates, events and segments of the flood given in Genesis 7 and 8.

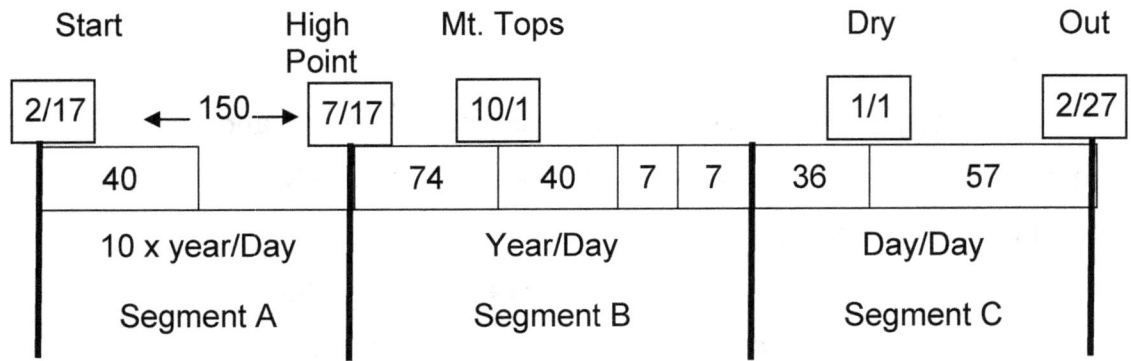

Figure17-1 FLOOD SEGMENTS

Segment A:

The flood begins on the 17th day of the 2nd month. The fountains of the deep overflow, the rain falls forty days and nights and the deluge, which rises to cover all the earth, reaches its highest point on the 17th day of the 7th month.

In just these few days and dates we find the promise of Jesus. Remember, history is prophecy. When Abraham is given the promise that …"*all peoples on the earth will be blessed through you*" (Genesis 12:3)… the books of Moses are still 450 years in the future. What 'scripture' did Abraham have (besides the direct revelation of God) to support his understanding? The only scripture Abraham had was the "oral" (but most probably written*) histories of Adam, Noah and Job.

[*Note: While no proof exists that Moses used 'source material' for Genesis, it is very plausible that he did so. My heart can easily believe that Shem had (and preserved) a written record of God's creation. (Methuselah, Shem's great grandfather knew Adam for over 240 years! And Shem knew Methuselah for almost 100 years!) The first five chapters of Genesis have the form, style and format common to ancient clay tablet records. That Shem would preserve, copy and treasure the Adamic history and the narrative of his father Noah and the great flood is very believable. Shem lived an additional 500 years after the flood. He must have told his survival story many times. He probably discipled Job and in his later years may have also witnessed to Abraham. For Abraham to have taken a copy of 'Adam' and 'Noah' (his family record) along with him on his journey to the Promised Land is very reasonable. [The story of Job may also have gone with Abraham. Ancient Syrian clay tablets of the early second millennium BC tell the story of 'Yob' and his trials.] In Egypt, Abraham comes upon modern writing. It is then an easy step to see the 'tablets' transferred to scrolls and these hallowed records then used by Moses to create the Genesis rendition. Again there is no proof for such documentation, but the technology existed, the formats match and it is a very reasonable act for Shem and Abraham to create and preserve a family record. (Don't we all?) When we add the divine nature of "creation" to the family history a permanent record of the fall and the flood become imperative!!]

Both the Adamic and Noahic narratives stress the 'seed' metaphor with which Abraham has now been entrusted. Jesus says: "Abraham saw my day". How? In a vision? Perhaps, but also in the days and dates of the flood.

It was on the 15th of Ziv the second month, when the Glory of the Lord first appeared to the Israelites in the Sinai Desert. The flood begins on the 17th of the second month. The 17th would be the 3rd day of an event that began on the 15th. Is the flood a prophetic portrayal of the 3rd day of the Glory of the Lord? Scripture is replete with references to the third day - all for the Glory of Jesus. We will see that this 3rd day theme is consistent throughout the flood narrative.

The flood rains persist for 40 days and nights and the waters rise until the 17th day of the 7th month. This is a period of 150 days. If we consider these two periods (40 days and 150 days) as <u>separate</u> prophecies and multiply by 10 we have a divine 10x year/day relationship. Therefore, from 2/17 to 7/17 is not simply 150 days but 1,500 years!!

1500 years was a prophetic message to Moses. We saw earlier that 1500 prophetic years were established to glorify the role of Jesus the Lamb in the Passover (Note Table 17.1)

1500	Prophetic years	1446BC	Passover
x [A]		+ 32AD	Crucifixion
1478	Solar years	1478	Years

Table 17.1 **1500 Prophetic Years**

So here we have our first prophecy of Jesus that is hidden in the flood events....1500 prophetic years to the true Passover sacrifice. But we also have our first problem. The "high point" of the flood is reached in the 7th month. But the Crucifixion was not in Tishri, the 7th month, but rather in Nisan the 1st month. Here we must recall God's command to Moses following the exodus that from now on Nisan (originally the 7th month) was to become the 1st month. (See Exodus 12:2)

By this process Moses advances the calendar year by six months. The 1st of Nisan becomes New Years Day for the religious calendar (the one used in this work) but for the civil community Rosh HaShanah (the head of the year) remained the 1st of Tishri.

Therefore Segment A for the days of Noah has two "aspects": one for 1/17 in Nisan and one for 7/17 in Tishri.

To devout Jews and Christians the 17th of Nisan is obvious: 1/17 is the feast of First Fruits and Resurrection Sunday - **the 3rd day**!! (of the Glory of the Lord!) That the 17th of Nisan is both the feast of the First Fruits (the day after the 1st Sabbath after Passover and Resurrection Sunday is seen in Table 17.2.

	Nisan					
Sun	Mon	Tue	Wed	Thu	Fri	Sat
10	11	12	13	**14** **Passover**	**15** **Sabbath**	**16** **Sabbath**
17 **1st Fruits**	18	19	20	21	22	23

Table 17.2 **Passover to First Fruits – Nisan 32AD**

The four High Holy Days of Passion week, shown in bold, are the 14th through the 17th. But our story really begins on the evening of the 13th. Jesus celebrates his last meal with the disciples on the evening of the 13th. John 13:1 says *"it was just before the Passover"*. It is, in fact, the day before the Passover. The evening meal that John describes starts with Judas' identification as the betrayer of Jesus (and his exit into the night) and ends in the Garden of Olives – this is clearly the last supper and it takes place "before the Passover".

Jesus is taken in the garden the night of the 13th – which is the night of the 14th by Jewish reckoning. In Genesis God ends the creation story for 'Day One' by saying: "The evening and the morning were the first day (Genesis 1:5b). Therefore to a Jew (and any believer) the night precedes the day. Therefore after supper on Wednesday (when Jesus is captured) is the start of the 14th of Nisan. Jesus is tried six times. He is taken before Annas, Caiaphas, The Sanhedrin, Pilate, Herod, and Pilate again. Then He is crucified on the morning of the 14th - the day of preparation (John 19:42) - preparation for the Passover meal (which will be eaten after sundown that night). [Note: "Preparation" also includes preparing the 'house' – it must be free of leaven (yeast) – sin. There must be no sin present when we eat the Passover! We must prepare our 'hearts' (house) to receive Jesus.]

Jesus is buried on late Thursday afternoon on the 14th of Nisan. The next day is a Friday the 15th and it is the first official day of Passover week. Therefore the 15th is a special Sabbath. (Leviticus 23:7) Saturday the 16th is the regular Sabbath of the week [which starts the countdown to Pentecost (See Leviticus 23:16)] and Sunday the 17th is the day of Resurrection and the Feast of First Fruits.

[Note: There appears to be a conflict between the synoptics (The Gospels of Matthew, Mark and Luke) and the Passover chronology recounted in John. The synoptics tell of Jesus eating the Passover meal and being crucified the next day – seemingly on the 15th. But Matthew 26:5 also states that the High Priest's did not want to crucify Jesus during the Feast for fear of the crowds. If Jesus dies on the afternoon of the 14th, then that evening is the 15th and it is a High Sabbath and "all must remain inside". It is Passover. To the Chief Priest this is crowd control. The next two days are Sabbaths, so by the time any crowds can gather to protest Jesus' crucifixion it is already the 3rd day. By this time everyone will have calmed down, or so the chief priests believed.

The apparent conflict between John and the synoptics (i.e., Was the 'Last Supper' the Passover meal?") is resolved by noting the language of Mark 14:12: *"on the first day of the Feast of Unleavened Bread when it was <u>customary</u> to sacrifice the Passover Lamb".*

Why would Mark say "<u>customary</u>"? Every Jew understood that the Lamb was killed on the afternoon of the 14th and eaten after sundown (on the 15th) The reference to "<u>customary</u>" is almost absurd. But the apparent conflict rests in the issue of "custom" versus "official rule". The calendar was in the hands of the Chief Priests and they choose to delay the "official" new moon of Nisan by one day so that all Israel would get the "official news" of New Moon by Temple messengers. [Remember from Chapter 2 that the temple priests delayed the official "New Moon" – they controlled the calendar.]

Imagine if "Independence Day" in the United States was officially moved to the first Monday in July thereby creating a "politically acceptable" three-day weekend. Some folks would still celebrate the 4th of July by "custom", but the whole nation would be off from work for the "official" Monday observance.

We have a similar case in Israel. Jesus (and I am sure many other religious conservatives) ate their Passover by the moon (God's clock) but the whole nation observed the Sabbath laws according to the official calendar as set by the High Priest. Jesus obeys the Scriptures and the ordinances established by earthly authority (which also comes from God). Matthew, Mark and Luke record what was "customary" and John records what was "official". There is **no** conflict.

Thus we see in the events of Noah's flood a prophecy of 1500 prophetic years from **the 3rd day of the Glory of the Lord** in the cloud to **the 3rd day of the Glory of the Lord** risen from the dead [2/17 of 1446BC to 1/17 of 32AD].

How would this help Abraham understand God's covenant of the coming of the seed? Well, God told Abraham that his descendants would be slaves 400 years (Genesis 15). Using the same divine multiplier of 10 applied to the 40 days (of cleansing) we see the 400 years as prophecy to Abraham.

If this approach seems "contrived" let's look at the results. We have 400 years of slavery and then 1500 years of Passover rehearsal for a total of 1900 prophetic years. We would convert this to solar years as follows:

$$\begin{array}{r} 400 \\ +1500 \\ \hline 1900 \text{ Prophetic years} \\ \times \text{ [A]} \\ \hline 1872.7 \text{ solar years} \end{array}$$

Exodus 12:40 tells us that the Jews left Egypt after 430 **years to the very day**. By subtracting the 430 years from the years of the promise to Abraham we have

$$\begin{array}{r} 1872.7 \\ -430.0 \\ \hline 1442.7 \text{ years to _____?} \end{array}$$

The math produces 1442.7 years - but 1442.7 years until what?? Until the Promise! Until the seed! **Until the Messiah!!**

The Exodus was in the spring of 1446BC. This would be expressed as

1445.7 BC solar. Going forward from 1445.7 BC the remaining 1442.7 years until 'The Promise' gives us exactly 3 years short of zero reference. (There's our "3" again!!) By Moses calendar this zero point would be the 15th of Nisan of 1 AD. But Moses was using a calendar that had the start of the year advanced by six months (see Exodus 12:2). For Abraham the "head of the year" would still be in Tishri. Therefore our zero reference would be back six months at the 15th of Tishri of 1 BC. Subtracting exactly 3 years from Abraham's calendar would give us the 15th of Tishri of 4 BC. This then is the date for the fulfillment of 'The Promise' - the Messiah - the birth of Jesus of Nazareth.

Our current calendar is off by four years. We know from Scripture that King Herod tried to kill the infant Jesus. But Josephus tells us that Herod died just after the lunar eclipse of 4 BC (October 6 4BC). Therefore Jesus must have been born at this time. In Chapter 3.7 we were able to show that the birth of Jesus was at the feast of Tabernacles, the 15th of Tishri, in the 7th lunar month. When the waters of Noah's flood reached their "high point" we also have the <u>second aspect</u> of Segment A - This high point is reached on the 17th of the 7th month. This again is another case of the 3rd day - Jesus is born on the 15th of Tishri at the beginning of Tabernacles and Noah's flood celebrates the 17th - the 3rd day of the Glory of the Lord's birth.

To Abraham the 17th is in the <u>seventh</u> month and **celebrates the 3rd day of the Glory of the Lord's birth** – this is the <u>first</u> aspect of Segment 'A'.

To Moses the 17th is in the <u>first</u> month (by God's order) and celebrates **the 3rd day of the Glory of the Lord's Resurrection** - this is the <u>second</u> aspect of Segment 'A'.

So we see a prophecy within a prophecy where a single date reflects a dual or compound significance. While it is a very complex structure, this "dual significance" or multiple aspect architecture also appears in the other prophetic segments, segments B and C.

Segment B

In Segment B we have 'a day equals a year' scale. The <u>first aspect</u> of Segment B goes from the birth of Jesus to the destruction of the Temple. We find this prophecy in Noah's flood narrative as follows:

The next event in the flood sequence after the 'high point' is the uncovering of the tops of the mountain(s). This happens on the 1st day of the 10th month. From the 17th day of the 7th month to the 1st day of the 10th month is 74 days. If these 74 days represent 74 prophetic years then we are looking at:

```
    74   Prophetic years
  X [A]
    72.9 Solar years
-    3.3 Birth of Jesus in Solar years
    69.6 Destruction of Israel (Ab 70 AD)
```

From history we know that the year 70 AD was the Great Diaspora for Israel - the destruction of Jerusalem and the burning of the Temple. But how can we know that this set of events is the piece of history to which the prophecy points? The answer is provided by the date given for the exposure of the mountain tops, the 1st day of the 10th month. In Appendix IV we will show that this day (the new moon of Tebeth) is the <u>precise date</u> for the key sin of the nation of Israel - the denial of Jesus as God/Messiah. This interpretation is also reinforced by the numbers in the subsequent sub-segments. Noah waits 40 days before sending out a raven (an unclean animal) and a dove (a clean animal). The 40 days represent the 40-year cleansing in the desert that Israel received for rejecting the Promise (land). This was a sin unto death for that generation. Here the rejection of Jesus produces an <u>exact replica</u> of that penalty as all Israel is destroyed along with the cultic temple. The acceptance of the raven (the dove did not return to the ark / righteous) and the refusal of the dove [the Holy Sprit at Pentecost] (it was rejected and returned to the ark / righteous) tells us that the nation of Israel is still unclean - seeking unrighteousness.

Seven days later Noah sends out the dove again and it returns with an olive branch - peace! This is the giving of the Holy Spirit (seven years later) to the Gentiles (through Cornelius). This happens in the 1st Sabbath year of the Church 38 AD and shows that God has made peace with the Gentiles. [To the Jews first, and also to the Gentiles.] Israel's refusal of the Holy Spirit (whose job it is to reveal Jesus) usher's in the "Times of the Gentiles", as shown in Figure 17.2 (Also see Chapter 13; Times of the Gentiles).

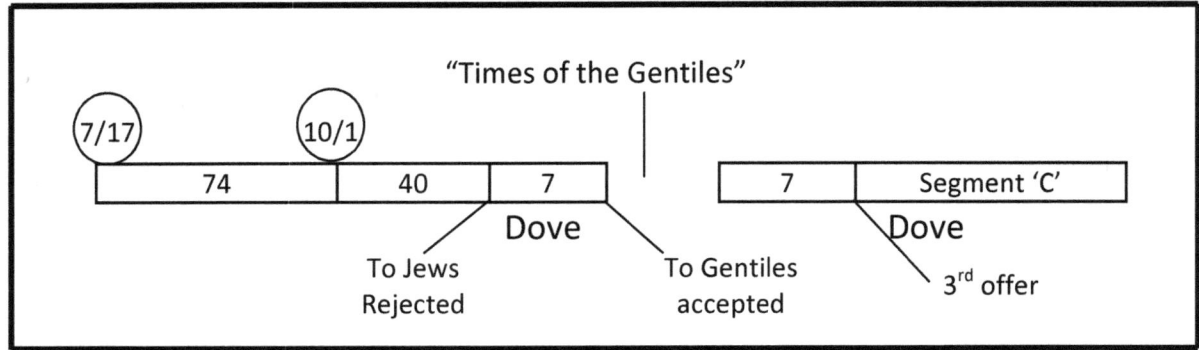

Figure 17.2 **Days of Noah; Segment 'B':**
Giving of the Holy Spirit

It is not until the Times of the Gentiles is fulfilled and the second 7 (the tribulation years) is completed, that the Holy Spirit is again offered to Israel. [This is Noah's third offering of the Dove... which is not refused!]

In our prior examination of Hosea's prophecy for the 'times of the Gentiles' (Hosea 6:2) we found the end of the age of grace at about 2008.5 lunar (fall 2009 solar).

Here in Noah's Prophecy we have a <u>double</u> refusal – the Jews refuse the testimony of Jesus <u>and</u> they refuse the witness of the Holy Spirit (who reveals Jesus), so the 40 years penalty unto death is multiplied by 7, according to Leviticus 26, and by 7 **again!!!**

To this product we add the 7 years (32 AD to 38 AD) that the Spirit was offered to the Jews. Thus:

$$40 \times 7 \times 7 \times [A] = 1931.8$$
$$+ 7$$
Years of double rejection $= 1938.8$

Since the penalty (delay of Promise) is appended to the destruction of the temple (and nation) we have:

```
      69.6   Destruction of Israel
   +1938.8   Rejection Delay
    2008.4   End time of the Gentiles Holy Spirit
```

This matches our initial estimate via the *'two days'* of Hosea almost exactly!

The remaining seven years in Segment B is the Tribulation, which ends when Noah sends out the dove again and it is accepted. Finally the Jews "see" Jesus as Messiah. These seven years are added to our previous result – thus:

> 2008.4 Start of Trib
> 7.0 Tribulation
> 2015.4 Jews see Jesus!

This projection of Segment B as the dual destruction of the temple and the nation of Israel is also quite complex. The first aspect is given in the prophetic holy years until the destruction of Israel for rejecting Jesus (70 AD) and the second aspect is found in 40 X 7 X 7 multiples for the rejection of the Holy Spirit. Both represent the destruction of the unrighteous for rejecting God and the forgiveness of God through Jesus.

Further support for this interpretation of the days of Noah is found in Segment C where the prophecy is 'day for day'. (See Figure 17.3)

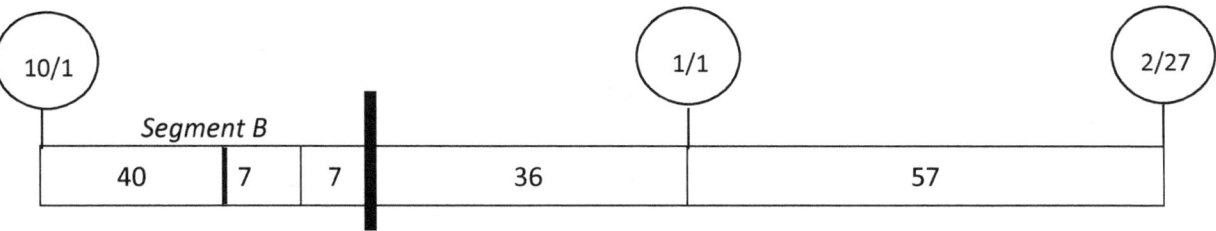

Figure 17.3 **The Days of Noah; Segment C**

To find the values in Segment C we must count the days from 10/1 (in Segment B) up to 1/1 and from 1/1 up to 2/27.

From 10/1 to 1/1 is 3 months or 90 days [remember a month is 30 days to Noah]. Fifty-four of these days are already used in segment B (40+7+7=54) so 36 days remain for Segment C.

From 1/1 to 2/27 is one month plus 27 days in month 2 for a total of 57 days in the final sub-segment.

We will apply these days of Segment C to the return of Jesus. Since we believe the entire Noahic flood prophecy is dedicated to the celebration of the **3rd day of the Glory of the Lord**, then the Prophecy will end with the 3rd day of Jesus' return – during the Angelic Harvest – the **3rd day of the Glory of the Lord.** (The return of the Glory of the Lord was examined individually in chapter 13.)

If day 2/27 is the 3rd day of the harvest, it is 3 Tishri 2016. [I further believe that it is on this day that the Glory of Jesus will be shown to the House of David (Zechariah 12:10)… "And they will look on me, the one they have pierced, and they will mourn for him as one mourns for an only child."] This will leave 7 days for the repentance of Israel before the completion of the harvest – these are the 'days of awe', which end on the 10th of Tishri 2016.

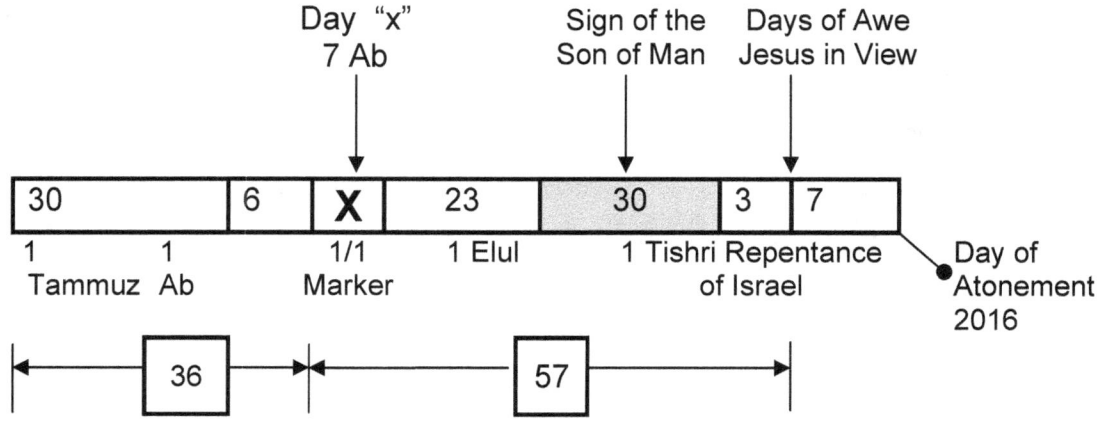

Figure 17.4
Days of Noah - The Last Days

The Last section of Segment C is 57 days. If we use the 1st of Tishri as a reference, then it is only 54 days back to the date that the Holy Spirit calls 1/1.

We must count backward from 1 Tishri (the first day of the Glory of the Lord) fifty-four days as follows:

```
  54
- 30    Days in Elul
- 23    Days in Ab
   1    Day X = the 7th of Ab
```

Our 54 days starts on the 7th of AB. This is the very day that Solomon's temple was destroyed in 586 BC (See 2 Kings 25:8) The Glory of the Lord left that temple and did not return until Jesus (The Lamb 32 AD) and until Jesus the King in 2016. [This Day "X" is also when the Romans sacked and destroyed Jerusalem in 70 AD. The destruction of Herod's temple was cited in segment B!!]

We note that the date for the segment C marker in Noah's prophecy is 1/1… the first day of a New Year, a new beginning.

The 36 days that precede the 1/1 new beginning marker are necessary to align Israel's 7-year covenant with Satan (Daniel 9:27) with the prophetic calendar. Since:

Seven Solar years = 365 ¼ x 7 = 2556 + ¾ = 2557 days

Seven prophetic years = 360 x 7 = 2520 + **36** + 1 = 2557 days

It is after this covenant expires (Daniel 9:27) that Satan, in a rage, will commit the abomination of desolation and thereby initiate the Sign of the Son of Man and the second coming of Jesus – as conquering King. After 30 days of signs in the heavens Jesus will sound the trumpet of God (shofar ha godal) on the 1st of Tishri and lead the Armies of Heaven in the final assault on Satan. On the 3rd of Tishri – **the 3rd day of the Glory of the Lord** – God will lift the veil from off the eyes of the Jews and they will see their Messiah – the one they have pierced.

From the 4th to the 10th of Tishri (7 days) the temple will be cleansed, anointed and rededicated to the Christ who, as High Priest, will conduct the ceremonies for the efficacious atonement of Israel on 10 Tishri 2016.

Thus we see from the days of Noah a detailed prophecy of the major redemptive events between God and man via **the 3rd day of the Glory of the Lord** – Table 17.3 is a summary of these events.

Day	Date	Jesus
2/17	1446 BC	Out of the Cloud
7/17	4 BC	Out of the Womb
1/17	32 AD	Out of the Earth
*7/3	2016 AD	Out of the Veil

*93rd day of Noahic prophecy; Segment C

Table 17.3 **The Third Day of the Glory of the Lord**

17B The Days of the Sons

In 2 Samuel 7, we find God's covenant with David. In this divine promise God assures David that his name will be great and that one of his sons will sit on the throne of Israel forever. [Not a bad promise!]

But on the surface there seems to be a problem. Since the God ordained captivity of Israel (in 586 BC) there's been no throne of Israel to sit upon!

Theologians agree that this covenant with David is a prophetic promise only truly realized in the Messiah (Jesus). However this covenant with David did have a physical component. Twenty-one descendants of David, from Solomon to Zedekiah, ruled Jerusalem from 970 BC (David's death) until the destruction of Jerusalem in 586 BC.

The only interruption to the reign of the House of David was the illegal reign of the usurper Athaliah, daughter of Ahab and Jezabel, who pretended from 841 to 835 BC. Through this illicit monarch we see the onslaught of Satan against God and His plan for Messiah. Athaliah attempts to murder all of David's descendants and thereby put an end to the house of David. But God working through the High Priest Jehoiada preserves the line (in the child Joash) and destroys Athaliah in the seventh year of her reign.

If we again claim history as prophecy, then we see in the Davidic Covenant yet another pointer to the Second Coming of Jesus – the true fulfillment of this covenant. Summing the years for the house of David (less Athaliah's reign) and multiplying by 7[A] shows us just when David's greater Son will sit on the throne of Israel forever:

```
   970   Death of David
  -586   Israel into captivity
   384   House of David
    -7   Reign of Athaliah
   377   Reign of House of David
 x   7A
  2601.1 Years to Greater Son
  -585.6 End of Zedekiah's Reign (fall of Jerusalem)
  2015.5 Begin Reign of King Jesus
```

Once again we have a direct prophecy (such as Hosea's *'two days'*) or historic imagery (such as David's presumptuous census) which points to the year 2016 (in fact Tishri of 2016) for the **fulfillment of the ages.**

If we have rightly interpreted these data as the Return of the Glory of the Lord - Jesus Messiah, then:

Praise God!

If we are incorrect in our interpretation and Jesus should tarry, then:

Praise God!

***"Let everything that has breath praise the Lord."* (Psalm 150:6)**

Appendix I

Error Analysis

In this appendix we will examine some of the "unknowns" associated with the prophecy assessments and extrapolations expressed in this work. This will be a simplistic approach to the Error Analysis issue rather than a rigorous mathematical effort. The control issues are clearly: Assumptions

a. If the interpretation of Scripture is correct <u>and</u>

b. The application of Leviticus 26 is appropriate <u>and</u> the

c. Anderson coefficient/lunar calendar methodology is valid

Then:

How accurate are the results we obtained (previously Tishri of 2016) and what is the viable range of possible predictions?

To find or answer we must carefully evaluate the accuracy of the "input data" on a case-by-case basis.

A 2-1 <u>Anderson's original work</u>

Anderson's original interpretation of Daniel 9:25ff that is the assignment of 483 years (69 x 7 periods of years) as 483 "prophetic Holy years" of 360 days each is not challenged here. Rather this work accepts (and hopefully verifies) that Anderson's interpretation was "rightly inspired" - and God given. That 483 years of 360 days each equates to 173,880 days is also accepted. The issue is whether or not Anderson found the correct starting point for the 20th year of Artaxerxes – 1 Nisan 445 BC.

In his work "Chronological Aspects of the Life of Christ" Hoehner challenges Anderson's selection of 445 BC as the starting point, for the challenge is based on an old prophetic calculation controversy in chronological studies: "How did the ancients count the years of a king's reign?" Was a king's "first year" when he succeeded to the throne or was this the "ascension year" (a partial year) and then the subsequent calendar year (full year) properly "his first year"?

The answer is not easy to ascertain because of a number of inconsistencies and cultural unknowns. Not only did each ancient culture (society) have their own approach, the modern reader does not know if a cross-cultural chronologist is using the standard methodology of the subject kings culture (is the same methodology as the foreign society being recorded) or if the history is written using the referential norms of the "recording culture".

Was Daniel's reference to the "twentieth year" according to the Babylonian counting system or the Hebrew standard? [Let's assume here for simplicity that they were different standards.]

Hoehner sees the twentieth year of Artaxerxes as 444 BC (not 445 BC) and therefore places the arrival of the Messiah (Jesus grand entry) as the Passover of 33 AD (vice Anderson's 32 AD). If Hoehner is correct what affect would it have on the prophecy extrapolations of this work.

A) Times of the Gentiles

The "Times of the Gentiles" began when Peter conveyed the Holy Spirit to Cornelius (See Chapter 13, Case 3 and Acts 10) This event happened after the Church had rest (Acts 9:31) The NIV Chronologers placed this event just after Paul's visit in 38 AD as the start date. This work then added he prophecy of Hosea 6:2 (two days = two thousand years) as follows:

```
   2000   Prophetic Holy years
   x  [A]
   1971.25 Biblical Lunar years
     37.25 Peter to Cornelius  (summer 38 AD)
   2008.5  Tishri of 2009
```

This gives us the end of the Times of the Gentiles (Age of Grace) and a return to Law - the start of the Tribulation.

```
   2008.5  Return to Law
   +  7.0  Tribulation years
   2015.5  Return of Jesus
```

Hoehner's choice of 33 AD would not affect this calculation except we also posited that the "Times of the Gentiles" began during the initial Sabbath year of the Holy Spirit. If Christ's Grand Entry was 10 Nisan 33 then Pentecost was in about May of 33 AD and the Sabbath year would begin in the summer of 39 AD (not 38 AD). This advances our entire calculation by 1 year. However our determination of 32 AD for the Grand Entry/Crucifixion/Pentecost is not without additional Scriptural support: See Noah's Prophecy.

B) Noah's Prophecy

Two 'aspects' of the Noahic prophetic schedules as interpreted here indicated 32 AD as the year of the crucifixion/Holy Spirit.

    i. The 150 days of rain were seen as indicating 1500 prophetic Holy years as a promise to Moses. This is from the symbolic Passover of the exodus to the true sacrificial Lamb of God (that Abraham said God would provide, in Genesis 22:8.) Note: No partial years or decimals are involved here because we are counting the recurrence of the prophetic Passover - so it is the number of rehearsals (an integer) that is counted (also see Chapter 17). Advancing from the symbolic first Passover (1446 BC) by 1500 prophetic holy years gives us:

$$\begin{array}{r} 1500 \\ \underline{[A]} \\ 1478 \\ -1446 \end{array}$$

32 AD for the year of the true Passover sacrifice.

The error range here is very wide because we are multiplying the "days of rain" by 10. If the actual period of rain was 149 ½ or 150 ½ days then our answer of 32 AD shifts by about ± 5 years. But surely the Holy Spirit knew this as well when He gave us 150 days (exactly?). However, we do find a second pointer to 32 AD in the same Noahic prophecy.

    ii. If our interpretation as to the significance of the date given as 10/1 for the mountain tops appearing (Genesis 8:5) correctly correlates to our proof of 10/1 as the date for Jesus' rejection by the Jews (New Moon Festival of the Feast of Dedication). And assuming again (using History as prophecy) that the penalties for the rejection of Jesus equate precisely to Mosaic penalties for rejection of the land...38.6 years... then at the mid-point of 70 AD we should see the end of this initial penalty period [which must end in death as it did at the time of Moses (Reject Jesus = death]. This is the destruction of the nation and the people on 9 Ab of 70 AD. Ab is the 5th lunar month so this destruction occurred at about 69.4 algebraically (Biblical lunar).

If the 74 days in the flood history from 7/17 to 10/1 is correctly interpreted as portraying the years from the arrival of the Promise made to Abraham (Birthday of Jesus 15 Tishri 4BC) until the Temple's destruction, then we have:

```
74     Prophetic Holy Years
[A]
72.9
-3.5   Birth of Jesus [by Mosaic calendar) Tabernacles of 4 BC
69.4   Destruction of Temple
```

Finer accuracy can be attempted here since actual days and dates are known, but accuracy to the month is adequate. If the destruction of the temple was precisely 38.6 years after the rejection of Jesus then:

```
69.4 AD  Destruction
-38.6    Penalty
30.8 AD  Rejection
```

30.8 algebraic equates to the 10th lunar month of 31 AD just as was required. Jesus was crucified 103 days later at the Passover of 32 AD (See Appendix 4, Table A4-1).

Hoehner's challenge to Anderson of 33 AD vs. 32 AD seems effective in a 'stand-alone environment', but this is not the case. Events in Scripture are not stand-alone but form part of a non-contradictory whole. Hopefully this work has shown that the prophecies are all inter related and fit together perfectly to make a flawless picture of Jesus...Scripture cannot be broken.

Anderson, therefore, stands correct in his placing the thirtieth year of Artaxerxes at 445 BC and the arrival of Messiah Jesus at the Passover of 32 AD.

A 2-2   Babylonian Captivity

In Chapter 7 we were able to show that the 70 years prophecy of Jeremiah was fulfilled precisely in the 69 years of actual captivity (605 to 536 BC). We know from Babylonian History that Nebuchadnezzar's defeat of the Egyptian army at Charchemish was early in the campaign of 605 BC. Therefore we are looking at late spring. (The time when kings go to war!) Also, while we do not know what day, nor do we know the month - Ziv - the second lunar month in 536 BC when the captivity prophetically ended (with the laying of the second foundation). Any uncertainty here is on what day in Ziv (536BC) or what month in the spring/summer of 605 BC. The variance would be -30 days if the battle of Charchemish were unusually early in the spring (e.g. If spring rains ended early that year) to about +90 days if the battle was fought in the late summer. Any error in the selection of the start date <u>does not</u> affect the subsequent prophetic extrapolations because that work was based on the known terminus date of Ziv 536 BC. Here the variance is ±15 days (the 1st of Ziv to the 30th of Ziv). Since the work of Grant Jeffrey's is based on only one-year accuracy, what day in the month of Ziv does not affect his work. We will, however, take a closer look at the affect of these ±15 days in Section A2-3 Israel in the land.

A 2-3 <u>Israel in the Land</u>

In Chapter 9 we discussed Grant Jeffrey's interpretation of the 430 year penalty as given to Ezekiel in Chapter 4 of his prophetic book. Jeffrey assumed that with 70 years served in captivity the remaining 360 were still applicable - that Israel was on probation. When Israel failed to obey God (in cleansing and rest) the 360 years was multiplied by 7 according to Leviticus 26:13, 18.

Jeffrey's math produced

```
      360    Prophetic Holy years Probation
    X 7[A]   Leviticus 26:13,18
     2483
    - 536
     1947    AD
      +1     No year zero
     1948    AD = Israel off probation, back in the land
```

Jeffery did not use algebraic expressions for dates so he had to correct the math by adding 1 year to 1947 to produce 1948 (The calendar goes from 1 BC to 1 AD. There is no "year zero".)

How accurate was the prediction of 1948? Our start date was in 536 BC, the foundation of the second Temple (Ezra 3:10). The birth of Israel was 14 May 1948, which was on the 5th day of the second month - the 5th of Ziv. Over a period of almost 2500 years we have accuracy to the month! Incredible!!

Algebraic Approach

If we <u>assume</u> the 18th of Ziv 536 BC (the 3rd day of the Glory of the Lord) for the foundation, this is - 535.86 (algebraic). Using [A] adjusted for <u>the 400 year century leap-year </u>(360/365.2425) then our standard calculation produces

```
        360
       x 7[A]
      2483.829
     - 535.864
      1947.965
```

This is the 5th of Ziv 1948...The birthday of Israel!!! An <u>exact</u> answer after 2500 years!! YES!! This is true <u>IF</u> ... <u>IF</u> the foundation date was on the 18th of Ziv. However I prefer the 17th of Ziv. This is the 3rd day of the Glory of the Lord (from Chapter 17). The one-day error would then be found in that the Gregorian calendar is 1 day too long in 3363 years. After 2500 years of our prophecy this calendar plan is detected in our rounding off to the nearest day. I'll vote for the 17th of Ziv the 3rd day of the Glory of the Lord! We can ask Him ourselves pretty soon!! Praise God!!

APPENDIX II

Penalty Brick 1 - Giants in the Land

From the algorithm $490 [A] = F\, 7^3$, we computed F as equal to 1.408 years. 1.408 years X 365.25 days/year = 514 days.

Starting at the Passover of 1446 BC, we can now find the time of year more accurately that the Scriptures call *'the season of the first ripe grape harvest.'*

The approach taken is idealistic (having alternating months of 29 then 30 days). We were not there to declare the day of the new moon - for the month of Ziv or Sivan, etc. It is possible for two or three consecutive new moons to all be 29 solar days apart or conversely, it is also possible for two or three consecutive new moons to all be 30 solar days apart. Alternating months of 30 and then 29 days however, works well over long periods of time (i.e. many years).

But what we can see is that the spies left about the full moon of Tammuz and returned near the end of Ab. Note that a second Adar is needed to keep the lunar year aligned with the early grape harvest which is usually in the fourth month.

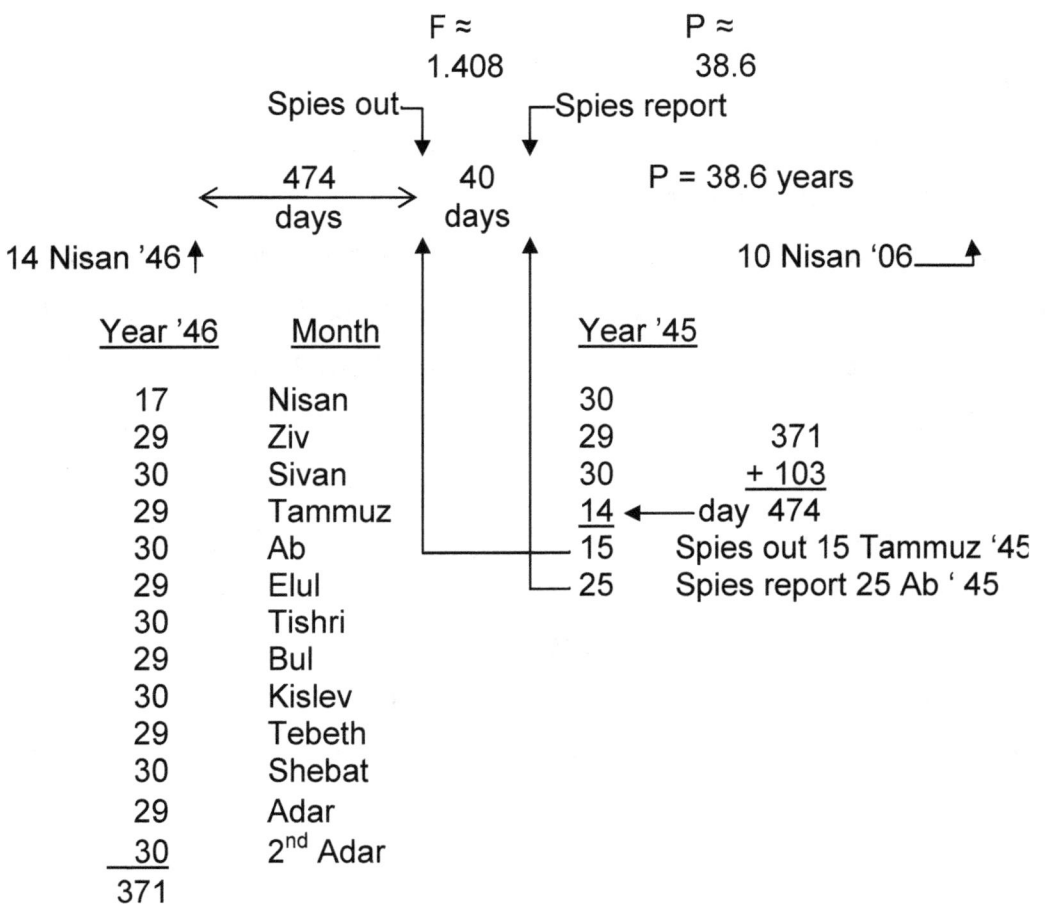

Table A2-1

SPIES OUT

We know that F = 1.408, but how many days is that?

365 x 1.408 = 514 days

Since the spies left 40 days earlier (514 - 40 = 474) we need to find out when was the 474th day after the Passover of 1446 BC. From Table A2-1 we see that this is the 15th of Tammuz. 40 days later would be the 25th of Ab.

APPENDIX III

Jesus denied and the Baptist beheaded

In Chapter 16 we posited the dedication feast rejection of Jesus as the sin event which defines the F + P = 40 penalty brick. That means the F segment began 514 days before the sin event. The terminus was estimated to be the new moon festival of the Chanukah feast week. This would be the very end of the month of Kislev (The night of the new moon for the 1st of Tebeth). Going backwards 514 days would bring us to the 19th of Ab 30. Our original estimate of 9 Ab 30 for the start of the 40-year period was very close. The 19th of Ab is within the 20 days of lunar/solar calendar float about the 9th of Ab test point.

It is a more difficult task to find out what single event marks the starting point for the F period. There is sufficient confusion about the length of Jesus' ministry (2½ years to 3½ years) to cloud the issue. It seems "reasonable" however, that the start point would be a **major event** in the history of Israel and in salvation history as well. There are not a lot of days or events between 28-32 AD that seem appropriate - and it would have to be an event about 1¾ years before the crucifixion (514 + 103 = 617 days, 617/365 = 1.7 yr. Recall from Chapter 16 that the F event is 103 days prior to the crucifixion). If the **three** Passovers of John's Gospel are correct (i.e. the Feast of John 5:1 **is not** a Passover), then Jesus' ministry was **about** 2½ years from Baptism (Fall 29) to Crucifixion (Spring 32). So 1.7 years prior to the crucifixion would be only 9½ months after Jesus was baptized - early in His walk - somewhere in the summer of 30 AD. The major event of this period is the execution of John the Baptist. [NOTE: I realize that I am open to much criticism here. I have never studied the arguments surrounding the chronology of Jesus' ministry - in fact, I welcome any reader's support or correction on this matter.]

The words and life of John (the Baptist) play a larger role in the Gospel of John than in the synoptics. There are the Baptist's denials in 1:19ff and the **two** Lamb of God, Son of God, references (found only in John) in 1:29-37. This is a powerful message. It is when the Baptist testifies that Jesus is the One, the **Son of God** that the disciples decide to follow Jesus. There are, at this time, only two

<u>witnesses</u> of this truth on Earth. Jesus and John. The Baptist proclaims what the Jews at the dedication **reject** - Jesus as the Son of God. The Gospel of John again emphasizes the Baptist's testimony in 3:22-36.

Here is my chronology of Jesus' life for the next 9 ½ months:

After His baptism and His cleansing/dedication (40 days in the Desert), Jesus goes to the 1st Passover of the three mentioned in John (John 2:12). Fittingly, Jesus cleanses the temple. He also teaches Nicodemus, performs signs for the people and heads home - passing through Samaria on the way (John 4).

Upon reaching Galilee, Jesus remarks that a prophet has no honor in his own country (John 4:44). This is surely still early in His ministry. He then raises the widow's son in Nain by Cana (Luke 7:15) (John also puts Jesus in Cana at this return from the temple cleansing – John 4:46), and Luke says "this news about Jesus spread throughout 'the land of the Jews!'" (Luke 7:17)

It is at this time, after just getting back in Galilee, that Jesus is visited by the Baptist Disciples and queried about *"are you the one?"* [Messiah Ben Joseph/Messiah Ben David or both?] Jesus says: *"Go back and report to John"* (Luke 7:22), so John is <u>alive</u> here - it is **after this** questioning that Jesus goes to Jerusalem for another feast (John 5). If this unnamed feast is another <u>Passover</u>, a <u>whole year</u> would have to have passed on Jesus' walk home! This just does not seem likely. This next feast is probably the Feast of the Tabernacles because Jesus' preaching has its emphasis on <u>water</u> and <u>light</u> - both major parts of the temple rituals at Tabernacles. Jesus now testifies to the truth of the Baptist's witness - but refers to him in the **past tense** (John 5:35). It is Chapter 6 of John that opens with another Passover.

If this chronology is correct, the Baptist was dead by Tishri of 30 AD - within 12 months of having baptized Jesus - our date of 19 Ab (for the start of the F period) is two months **prior** to Jesus' witness of John being dead by the Feast of Tabernacles (30 AD). Thus Herod beheaded John c 19 Ab 30 AD.

So we have our beginning and our end - it is John the Baptist who announces and proclaims that Jesus is the Son of God (John 1:34, 3:35) and it is the Jews who declare this message blasphemous...that Jesus, a mere man, should claim to be God (John 10:33). Figure A3-1 depicts these events.

With the death of John the Baptist, the last prophet, the Old Testament book is spiritually closed 19 Ab 30 AD.

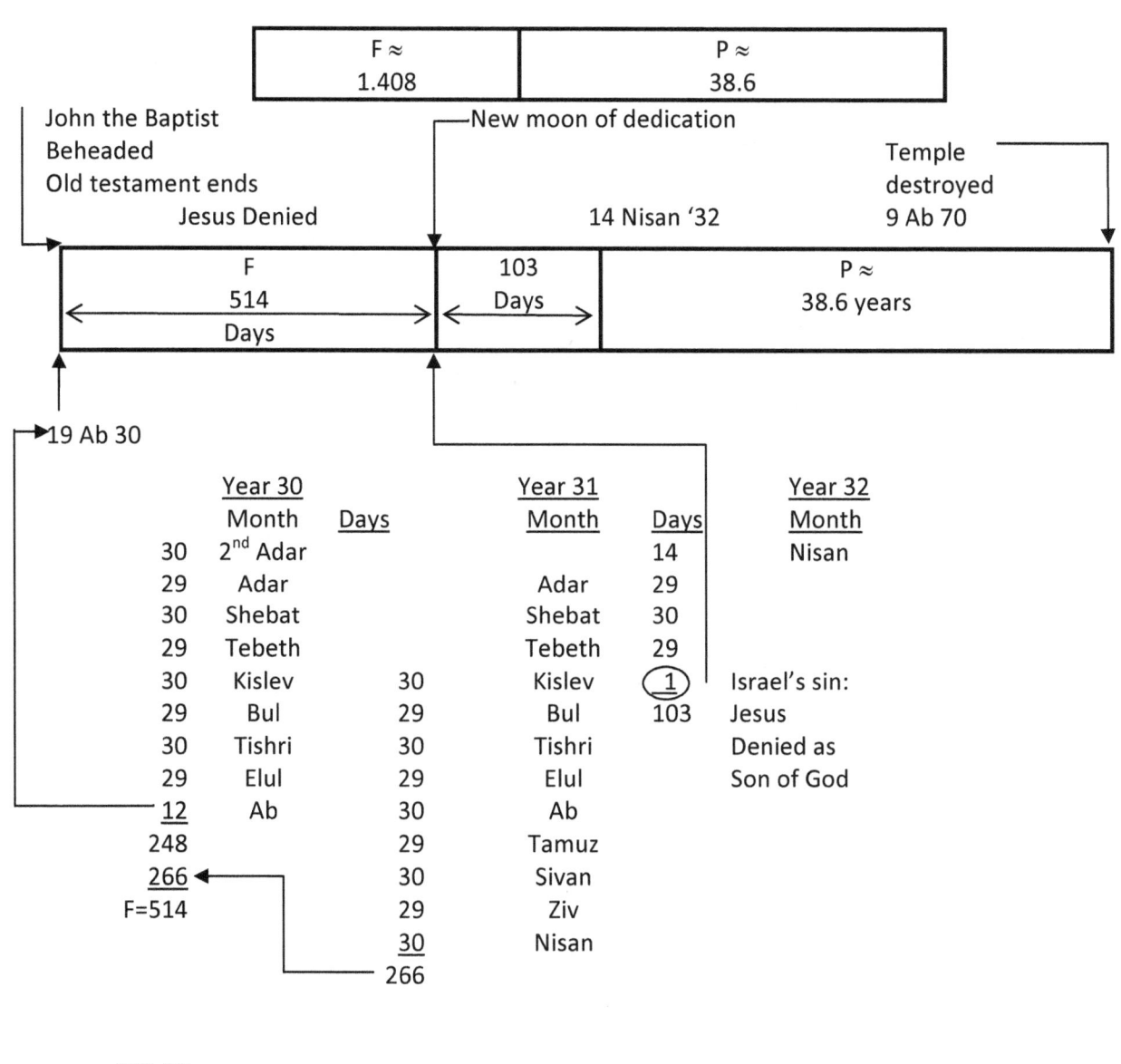

Table A3-1

JESUS AND THE BAPTIST

APPENDIX IV

50 and 50 again

We have seen the Jews miss two potential Jubilees - two attempts to enter the Kingdom. Each failed attempt is marked with an Ebenezer as a stone witness. These were the foundations of the first and second temples. Each of these 50-year periods has an associated 50-day parallel.

The first 50 days is from First Fruits to Sinai to receive the Law, the Ten Commandments. This is determined as follows:

$17^{th} - 30^{th}$	Nisan	=	14 days
$1^{st} - 30^{th}$	Ziv	=	30 days
$1^{st} - 3^{rd}$	Sivan	=	3 days
	Total	=	47 days

Note: We have two consecutive months (Nisan and Ziv) of 30 days each. While uncommon, it is possible - the plus or minus 13 hour variation in the lunar orbit allows for this occurrence. It was required in 1446 BC because 17 Nisan, 15 Ziv and 6 Sivan are all Sundays! (See Table A4-1)

The three days in Sivan is found in Exodus 19:1. The Israelites reached Sinai in the third month (Sivan) "<u>on the very same day</u>." This unusual expression in Hebrew tells us the <u>number of the day</u> was the same as the <u>number of the month</u> - so it was on the third day of the third month. This gives us 47 days to the journey thus far. God then commands three days of purification/consecration to the Lord, thus 50 total days. Exodus 19:16, 17 tell us "**on the third day....**Moses led the people...to meet with God."

NISAN 1446 BC

S	M	T	W	TH	F	S
					1	2
3	4	5	6	7	8	9
10	11	12	13	14 Passover	15 Exodus	16 Start
17 First Fruits	18	19	20	21	22	23 1st
24	25	26	27	28	29	30 2nd

Ziv 1446 BC

S	M	T	W	TH	F	S
1	2	3	4	5	6	7 3rd
8	9	10	11	12	13	14 4th
15 1st Glory	16	17	18	19	20	21 5th 1st Sabbath
22	23	24	25	26	27	28 6th
29	30					

Sivan 1446 BC

S	M	T	W	TH	F	S
		1	2	3	4	5 7th
6 Pentecost						

Table A4-1

SPRING 1446 BC

Moses ascends the mountain to meet with God (up close and personal) for 40 days and nights. The people, however, can't wait. They build the infamous golden calf - choosing a god of this world (what was in their heart) over the Creator - they were in bad need of cleansing (us too?).

The second 50 days comes when they leave Sinai for the Kingdom (still unclean). The Jews left Sinai on the 20th of Ziv. They travel just three days and start to complain - the people of this world - pagans who thought they wanted to leave Egypt - started this complaining process. But it got worse (a little leaven!).

In Numbers 12, both Aaron and Miriam talk against Moses. God sends leprosy on Miriam. Moses pleads (intercedes) with God on their behalf and God relents - but seven days are spent waiting for Miriam's cleansing.

The people move on and reach the Kingdom's border in the season of the "first ripe grape harvest." This, we have seen, was about the 14th day of Tammuz. Thus we have:

20-29 Ziv	=	10 days
1-30 Sivan	=	30 days
1-14 Tammuz	=	14 days
		54 Total days

If we subtract the seven days delay for Miriam's cleansing, we have

$$\begin{array}{r} 54 \\ -7 \\ \hline 47 \text{ days} \end{array}$$

It is **reasonable** that another three-day consecration would have been required for a total of 50 days. But the Jews, still with unclean hearts, plunged right in.

They didn't ask God, they just held a meeting and decided to spy out the land. Alas, it might have gone differently. If we add the 3-day ritual for cleansing, we see that this second sojourn was also a 50-day trip. Both of these trips failed to cleanse Israel - so God cleansed that generation - they perished in the wilderness. We can see these same 50 days replayed in the 50-year monuments/Jubilees - the two foundations.

Finally on the third Jubilee (2016) **Jesus will lead his people into the Kingdom.**

APPENDIX V

Days in the Desert

We read in Chapter 12 of the Revelation that the 'red dragon with seven heads and 10 horns' will attempt to devour 'the child' (Jesus) of the 'woman clothed with the sun'. While there exists in theological circles continuing debate over the identity of "the woman" this text will consider her to be the believing remnant of the Nation of Israel. Therefore as an Old Testament body of true Messianic believers the woman is covered by God's mercy and is sheltered from Satan during the last half of the Tribulation. This divine protection is for 1,260 days (42 months) at a place in the desert prepared for her by God.

This period of 1260 days is blessed indeed. The period begins 60 days after the termination of the daily sacrifice and continues up to the 10-day angelic harvest of 2016 AD, Yamin Nora'im, the days of awe! This harvest begins on the Feast of Trumpets (1 Tishri) and continues to Yom Kippur the Day of Atonement. Since the last day of divine protection is the day before Trumpets, the total period begins 1,260 days earlier. This starting point can be found by the following

a) Since 1 Nisan to 1 Tishri (2016 AD) is exactly half a lunar year there are

$$\frac{354}{2} = 177 \, days$$

b) 1 Nisan 2013 to 1 Nisan 2016 is

$$\begin{array}{r} 354 \\ \times 3 \\ \hline 1062 \text{ Days} \end{array}$$

c) The inclusion of one 30 day Second Adar (13th month) for solar/lunar calendar alignment.

Therefore, summing the days we find

$$\begin{array}{r} 177 \\ 1062 \\ +30 \\ \hline 1269 \text{ Days} \end{array}$$

But the period of protection is for 1260 days not 1269. Therefore the divine protection begins <u>after</u> nine days in 2013 or on

> **The 10th of Nisan!**

The Messianic believers, like the children in Goshen, received the protection of the blood of the Lamb starting on 10th of Nisan - **INCREDIBLE!!**

EPILOGUE

We have seen in this text how amazing the details of Scripture are. Who knows what other mysteries are hidden in the <u>seemingly meaninglessness</u> of Scripture detail. I encourage all serious lovers of the Word to examine the minute details that the Holy Spirit may illuminate so that all the Glory of God's Word might be revealed - to the Glory of Christ JESUS = MARANATHA!

RJL

A Bit About the Author and the Writing of this Book
By Ronald Woodfin, Ph.D., the author's Pastor

Following a series of difficult events in Roger's life, he had the opportunity to spend time at a retreat in Colorado. During this time, Roger realized the importance of surrendering his life into God's hands. He vigorously grasped the guidance and wisdom of the Holy Spirit. When he returned he was baptized in a friend's swimming pool. Roger was a new man.

Roger began regular and intense Bible study. The depth of his grasp of spiritual concepts and the entire revelation of scripture was amazing. His questions challenged me and required me to do a lot of homework of my own. He became a major participant in the life of the Church.

One of the most visible changes in Roger's life was his newfound desire to worship. Anyone who leads public worship is filled with joy when they see someone who can become lost in their private worship in the midst of the crowd.

Most people find it difficult to concentrate so much on God that they lose sight of themselves. Roger became an inspiration to our congregation because he truly worshipped whenever he could. It was clear that the songs, old or new, whatever the quality of the music, were a vehicle to transport him in a most vivid way into the very presence of God.

After a few months, Roger accepted a temporary transfer with his company to a position in the Washington area. The church had intermittent contact with him for that year but we learned he was spending almost all his available time in concentrated Bible study. He returned with a vision and clearly had God's call to a special task. He began immediately to walk in the light he had. Roger used what resources he had to begin a mission called "Gadarenes". He said this was for a personal testimony, because he identified with what the demoniac had gone through. He said that he had been freed from many things and could now sit at the feet of Jesus. The ministry was first conceived to be a free Christian school. It was dedicated to teaching unemployable people who had dropped out of high school.

Roger rented a house in one of the most poverty stricken and crime filled areas of Albuquerque known as "The War Zone". It quickly became apparent that most of his prospective clients were hungry much of the time, so he started feeding them. He even remodeled the house and garage to provide sleeping quarters for a dozen or so men. He lived there in the house with these people and showed them Jesus' love. He had no regular support for this work from any established group. A few churches contributed a little, but mostly he just prayed and asked God for support. As the mission grew, he needed something productive for his clients to do. He began to make muffins and sell them to office workers at coffee break time. Still, most of his funds came as miraculous answers to prayer.

This continued for some time. With regular Bible teaching and discipline, a number of people found new life in Jesus. Many more were helped in other ways. Through a series of circumstances, which seemed like opposition at the time, the Lord moved the ministry to Belen, New Mexico, a few miles south of Albuquerque. In retrospect, this was clearly God's direction to open new fields of work for Roger and the mission.

Near Belen is a state penal facility. Roger began working with inmates there and acquired the vision for Gadarenes next phase of work. He realized the need for a "half-way house" for prisoners being paroled, a place where they could readjust to non-prison society, and get their lives restarted in a proper direction. Roger knew from experience that Jesus could change a life, but he had no place to safely house those released to him. Even in the small town of Belen, the drugs, by which most of them got into trouble in the first place, were too readily available.

A few miles south of Belen is the tiny settlement called Bernardo. Through a variety of circumstances, Roger was able to purchase some property near there. He called it Morningstar Ranch. Roger moved the ministry there. It now houses staff, who must raise their own support, and a number of recently paroled clients.

There are some exciting success stories among the clients, several of whom have dedicated themselves to continuing the work with new clients. There are disappointments as well since many want to use the ministry only for their way out of prison. Whatever their past, Roger loved the men and cared for them as a father would his own children. He interceded with authorities, counseled the clients, and forgave them when they stole from him. He prayed with them, helped them get off drugs, and led a number to faith in Christ.

In November of 1997, Roger received word of his mother's severe medical condition and went to visit her in North Carolina. He became sick on the trip and was hospitalized when he arrived. Within a matter of weeks, his mother recovered completely and he was called home to spend eternity with Jesus.

Roger's death did not mean the death of Gadarenes Ministry. The half way house work has continued under the direction of Mike Crutchfield, one of the former clients of the ministry. Presently, the men do bake sales and have a moving business as a means of support. Roger's death also inspired the beginning of the Roger F. LaRose Food Bank in Sandia Park, New Mexico. This work feeds many families each week with the same generosity that Roger demonstrated when he was on the earth.

The proceeds from the sale of this book go to support the work of Gadarenes Ministry. It is our prayer that Roger's work will continue in his absence. We thank you for your interest and we pray that your life will be improved as a result of being touched by what God has done in His servant's life.

Editor's note: Since the original writing, Gadarenes Ministry merged with The Shepherd's Fold Ministry, Incorporated which later became Peace of Mind Training Institute, a tax-exempt organization. Peace of Mind Training Institute produces seminars and materials designed to help people experience Peace of Mind in every area of life. The proceeds from the sale of Jesus My King are used to provide scholarships for those who need financial assistance in order to receive the training they need and desire. The Food Bank is no longer in operation.

www.ingramcontent.com/pod-product-compliance
Lightning Source LLC
Chambersburg PA
CBHW081222170426
43198CB00017B/2691